Macmillan Building and Surveying Series

Series Editor: Ivor H. Seeley
Emeritus Professor, Nottingham Trent University

Quantity Surveying Practice Ivor H. Seeley
Recreation Planning and Development Neil Ravenscroft
Resource and Cost Control in Building Mike Canter
Small Building Works Management Alan Griffith
Structural Detailing, second edition P. Newton
Sub-Contracting under the JCT Standard Forms of Building Contract Jennie Price
Urban Land Economics and Public Policy, fifth edition Paul N. Balchin, Gregory H. Bull
and Jeffrey L. Kieve
Urban Renewal – Theory and Practice Chris Couch
1980 JCT Standard Form of Building Contract, second edition R.F. Fellows

Series Standing Order

If you would like to receive future titles in this series as they are published, you can make use of our standing order facility. To place a standing order please contact your bookseller or, in case of difficulty, write to us at the address below with your name and address and the name of the series. Please state with which title you wish to begin your standing order. (If you live outside the United Kingdom we may not have the rights for your area, in which case we will forward your order to the publisher concerned.)

Customer Services Department, Macmillan Distribution Ltd
Houndmills, Basingstoke, Hampshire, RG21 2XS, England.

Environmental Management in Construction

Alan Griffith

MSc, PhD, MCIOB, MIMgt

MACMILLAN

First published 1994 by
THE MACMILLAN PRESS LTD
Houndmills, Basingstoke, Hampshire, RG21 2XS
and London
Companies and representatives throughout the world

ISBN 0-333-60797-X

A catalogue record for this book is available
from the British Library.

Copy-edited and typeset by Povey–Edmondson
Okehampton and Rochdale, England

Printed in Great Britain by
Mackays of Chatham PLC
Chatham, Kent, England

To Michela

Acknowledgements

My appreciation is extended to Professor Ivor H. Seeley, the Series Editor, for reading through and commenting extensively on the draft typescript. Also, my thanks to Mrs Elasaid McLean for producing the text and graphic material.

Contents

Preface

Organisations of many kinds, perhaps none more so than those within the construction industry, are increasingly aware of the growing need to mitigate the potentially harmful effects of their business upon the environment. Environmental management is specifically concerned with environmental protection and environmental performance through managing the environmental effects of an organisation's business. Environmental management encompasses those aspects of policy, strategy, procedures and practice that form the organisation's response to its environmental situation.

A formal and structured approach to environmental management is essential in demonstrating, with assurance, that an organisation complies with current policy and legislation but, moreover, that it is committed to actively addressing environmental issues. The vehicle for this is the environmental management system, one that follows BS 7750: Specification for Environmental Management Systems. Such a system not only reflects an appropriate environmental management response but prepares the organisation for likely involvement in environmental assessment or auditing schemes, an increasing demand in many sectors of business today.

The construction industry has always had an unequivocal and considerable effect upon the environment but increasing concern in many quarters and specifically more stringent legislation means that environmental management will become a consideration central to its constitution and activity. Every organisation within the construction industry must take cognisance of its environmental situation.

Presented in three main sections, this book sets out to provide an insight into the concept of environmental management and its systems.

Part A presents an introduction to environmental management, outlining the management concepts and its importance in business today. Part B examines environmental management system development, highlighting appropriate specifications, detailed requirements of a system and developing a system within an organisation. Part C focuses upon the practical application of environmental management within the construction industry, taking the concept through development, briefing, design and contract administration processes.

From the outset, environmental management can only be realised if the many and diverse factors that contribute to the construction process are brought together and, moreover, only if construction professionals pursue environmental management with integrity and commitment. Successful environmental management cannot and will not happen by itself.

Alan Griffith

Part A:
Environmental Management:
Introduction

1 Environmental Management

1.1 Introduction

Strong and developing awareness of environmental issues has, for some considerable time, put increasing pressure on commercial and, in particular, manufacturing and industrial organisations to improve their environmental standards. More generally, organisations of many kinds are more conscious of the need to mitigate any adverse effects of their business. Their perception is twofold, first in the expectation of increasingly stringent governmental legislation at both national and international levels, second in response to increasing intolerance and concern demonstrated by the general public for environmentally unsound business practice. No longer can any organisation be in ignorance of, or simply choose to ignore, environmental, or what are often termed 'green', issues.

With developing environmental awareness, some organisations have conducted preliminary environmental reviews of their activities. Such intra-organisational environmental assessments have provided, as one would expect, predominantly introspective operational analysis. For an organisation to plan, monitor and control the environmental effects of its business, detailed review must be undertaken within an authoritative and recognised structured management framework, an environmental management system.

A blueprint for establishing an environmental management system is presented by BS 7750: Specification for Environmental Management Systems.[1]

This standard presents a specification for and guidance to any organisation seeking to develop an environmental management system. BS 7750 is designed to enable any organisation to formulate and implement an appropriate management system as a basis for ensuring effective environmental performance of their business practices. Moreover, it prepares an organisation for likely involvement in environmental assessments or auditing schemes, an increasing demand in many sectors of business today.

The framework of BS 7750 draws upon BS 5750,[2] the UK's national standard for quality assurance systems, and its European and international QA counterparts EN 29000 and the ISO 9000 series of standards. In addition, BS 7750 was developed to complement European Community (EC) environmental legislation. As BS 7750 shares common management systems principles with BS 5750, an organisation may, if appropriate and with care, adopt an existing management system which conforms with BS 5750 as a basis for an appropriate environmental management system although there are some differences in detail which must be accommodated within the environmental management system.

An environmental management system, conforming to BS 7750, enables any organisation to develop with futurity an environmental ethos which encapsulates their business policy, objectives and procedures with respect to their interaction with the environment. Environmental management systems are essential to demonstrating sound and acceptable environmental performance and, moreover, in satisfying the wider concerns for environmental issues.

1.2   The concept of environmental management

Environmental management and environmental management systems are specifically concerned with environmental protection and environmental performance. They address the *environmental effects* of an organisation's business.

Environmental effect

Organisations interact with the environment in many ways and to varying degrees and the effects can, be direct or indirect, be adverse or beneficial, be vague or manifest. Almost all organisations are likely, at some time, to affect the environment in which they exist. *Environmental Management* is therefore fundamental to nearly all organisations.

Environmental management

Environmental management encompasses those aspects of policy, strategy, procedures and practice that form the organisation's response to its environmental situation. An organisation implementing environmental management is charged with critically examining their activities in response to any potential threat that they may hold to the environment. It must do this within its organisational framework by developing a formal environmental management system. Whilst the establishment of an environmental management system may appear to be a daunting proposition to most organisations initially, in fact an environmental management system places no greater demands upon an enterprise than the basic prerequisites of sound organisation and competent management. Like most concepts it must be perceived by them as a challenge and commitment to organisational development and opportunity and not a demonstrative burden.

1.3   Importance of environmental management

Greater awareness of environmental standards, environmental management and environmental management systems is important for a number of reasons:

- Growth in the 'green movement' at local, national and international levels increasingly puts pressure on all industries to produce more environmentally acceptable outputs.
- The public is increasingly intolerant of environmentally unsound business practice. The use of natural resources, pollution and recycling are prominent examples exemplifying public concern.
- National, European and international legislation dictates that industries of all kinds must take account of environmental protection for their business to be acceptable in the marketplace.
- It allows organisations to demonstrate that their activities meet recognised and authoritative environmental guidelines.

A formal and structured approach to environmental management is essential in demonstrating, with assurance, that an organisation complies with current policy and legislation and furthermore, is committed to broader environmental issues.

There is little doubt that the commercial marketing benefits of demonstrating the use of a recognised and authoritative environmental management system are considerable. In the same way that compliance with BS 5750: Quality Assurance Systems, is a recognised '*hallmark*' of an organisation's commitment to quality of service or product, so demonstration of commitment to environmental management will become prerequisite. In addition, it is well accepted that certification to an appropriate quality assurance scheme is frequently used as a pre-selection criterion by those procuring products or services, so likewise the recognition of an organisation that demonstrates environmental management may be essential to an organisation's trading position in the marketplace.

Certainly, an organisation should gain a significant competitive edge. In the short term this is likely to be realised in terms of organisational efficiency and effectiveness with the self-satisfying knowledge that one's business practice is mitigating potentially adverse environmental effects. In the medium to longer term, advantages are likely to ensue from enhanced investor and customer confidence and the associated trading benefits that this can bring.

1.4   What is an environmental management policy and strategy?

An environmental policy is fundamental to the development of the environmental management system. It sets out the organisation's intentions from executive level and forms the basis for organisational aims, objectives and procedures. In essence, an environmental policy represents the public face of an organisation's environmental response. It is a published statement of the intentions of the organisation in relation to its environmental effects.

Because all organisations are diverse and individual, even unique, an organisation must define for itself the criteria that form the basis of its environmental policy. Also, all organisations are subject to change and, therefore, those criteria forming the policy need to be all-embracing, yet retain sufficient flexibility to accommodate fluctuations in, for example, its: aims; objectives; procedures; technology; and marketplace. If an organisation's environmental policy is too narrow in scope it is likely to be ineffective, failing to determine realistic aims and objectives, whilst one that is over ambitious may be impossible to implement in practice.

An organisation's environmental policy must therefore be formulated around the company's core business and accurately reflect the business objectives and targets within safe measures of protection to the surrounding environment. Compiling an appropriate environmental policy is the first step in commitment towards organisational strategy and activity for environmental management.

1.5   What is an environmental management system?

An environmental management system is an organisation's formal structure, encompassing procedures, practices, resources and processes, that implements environmental management.

BS 7750 provides an organisation with guidance on the specification for and implementation of an environmental management system. Within the standard, an organisation has sufficient flexibility to evolve its own individual policies, strategies and objectives to implement an environmental management system that bests suits *the* organisation. Environmental management systems can therefore be developed and implemented by almost all organisations, irrespective of their business or biographical orientation.

To maximise the use of an environmental management system, its concepts must be viewed from a number of perspectives. An environmental management system may, at a primary level, facilitate improvement within the organisation, for example by making energy savings within the work environment. At a second level it may review organisational operations to reduce wastage or encourage recycling of resources. At a third level environmental management systems can promote an organisation's image in the commercial marketplace through environmental protection assured in the course of providing its services or products. An environmental management system should therefore seek to address the environmental effects of its practices both within and outside the organisation.

1.6 To whom is environmental management relevant?

Environmental management is relevant to any organisation who truly wishes to:

- Recognise the environmental effects of its business.
- Demonstrate its commitment to environmental protection.
- Assure itself of compliance with stated environmental philosophy and policy.
- Demonstrate such compliance to a national and international audience.
- Recognise growing concern for environmental issues.
- Accommodate increasingly stringent environmental and associated legislation.
- Be prepared for environmental assessments, auditing and certification schemes.

Increasing awareness of the need for environmental management is an implication of the many inefficiencies and difficulties experienced by organisations in the wider undertaking of their business; also, in the way organisations perceive the environment and their conflicting moral and commercialised regard for it.

Environmental management is relevant to: clients; investors; insurers; consumers; legislative and regulatory bodies; environmental control agencies; environmental protection groups; employers; employees; and the public.

As all organisations are likely, at some time in the future, to respond to the generally increasing concerns for environmental performance and environmental protection, so the concept and practices of environmental management will become more relevant to their organisation. They may find that proactive participation in environmental management is simply prerequisite, not only to their level of competitiveness but to their very survival in the marketplace. Management, in all organisations, must take cognisance of environmental issues. If it should choose not to, it does so at its own peril.

References

1 British Standards Institution (BSI), BS 7750: *Specification for Environmental Management Systems* (1992).
2 British Standards Institution (BSI), BS 5750: *Quality Systems* (1979, revised 1987).

Part B:
Environmental Management:
System Development

2 Environmental Management Specification

2.1 Specification for environmental management systems

Specification for environmental management systems is presented in BS 7750.[1] This standard specifies the basic requirements for the formulation, development, implementation and maintenance of an environmental management system directed towards compliance with an organisation's stated environmental policy and objectives.

BS 7750 also provides guidance on the specification and implementation of an environmental management system within existing management systems of an organisation.

The elements specified in BS 7750 are essentially generic and can therefore be incorporated into the environmental management system of any organisation. The inclusion of these elements will, obviously, differ among organisations as environmental policy, objectives and procedures will vary from organisation to organisation.

The standard does not present specific criteria for environmental performance. Such criteria must be determined by an organisation itself given the almost certain variance in nature, composition and situation that exists among all organisations. Guidance on the acceptable levels of environmental management performance is available in complementary documentation, designed to be consulted in association with BS 7750. These take the form of specific sector application guides or may be published as British Standard Codes of Practice (CP).

An organisation may wish to use an existing management system as its basis for developing its environmental management system. BS 5750: Quality Systems[2] may be used in this respect and can be extended to meet the specification of BS 7750. BS 7750 environmental management systems share generic management system principles with BS 5750 and therefore comply with European and international standards EN 29000 and ISO 9000.

BS 7750 was developed to complement the European Community (EC) Eco-Management and Auditing Scheme and therefore specifies the requirements for an environmental management system that meets the registration criteria of their scheme. The Eco-Management and Audit Scheme establishes a registration process in which participating companies are required to demonstrate their commitment to environmental protection by maintaining an environmental management system within their organisations. In addition,

11

environmental management systems developed to these specifications meet the requirements for satisfying national and international environmental auditing, the implications of which are reviewed in a later chapter.

2.2   Environmental management systems: structure

Structure for an environmental management system is based on the premise that an organisation shall develop, implement and maintain an appropriate management system for ensuring that the effects of organisational activity conforms to its stated environmental policy, aims and objectives and which in so doing, meets current environmental protection legislation. To achieve this, the organisation must demonstrate unequivocally that it meets a number of specific requirements. These follow in section 2.5 and are illustrated in Figure 2.1.

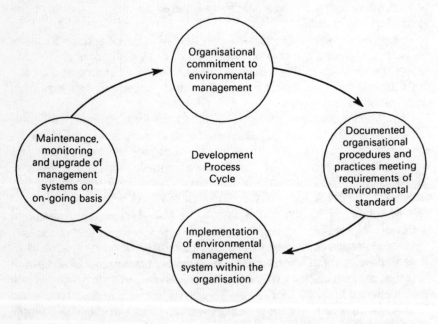

Figure 2.1 Organisational development process cycle for an environmental management system

While BS 7750 encourages the use and modification of an existing organisational management system such as BS 5750, to form the basis of an environmental management system, it does require the organisation to address its structure of activities within the following systems elements:

- Environmental policy.
- Organisation and personnel.
- Environmental effects.
- Environmental objectives and targets.
- Environmental management programme.
- Environmental management manual and documentation.
- Operational control.
- Environmental management records.
- Environmental management audits.
- Environmental management reviews.

Activities within these areas of organisation must be considered even if an existing similar management system is being used within the organisation. A structure based on these aspects will reflect the organisation's overall philosophy, aims and objectives towards environmental management.

The specific detailed requirements for system structure are presented in BS 7750: Specification for Environmental Management Systems,[1] and the reader is directed to this authoritative guidance document. Generic yet detailed guidance to environmental management systems development follows in Chapters 3 and 4. The broad structure outlined is represented in Figure 2.2.

2.3 Environmental terminology: definitions used in environmental systems specification

Before proceeding, in section 2.4 and Chapter 3, to develop the detailed requirements of an environmental management system, it is pertinent to define some aspects of environmental terminology.

Environment
> *The environs and conditions in which the organisation exists and functions.*

Environmental Effect
> *The effects of organisational activity upon its environs whether direct or indirect, detrimental or beneficial.*

Environmental Management
> *The aspects of policy, strategy, procedures and practice that form the organisation's response to its environmental situation in the course of its business.*

Environmental Management System
> *The organisation's formal structure that implements environmental management.*

Environmental Policy
> *A published statement of organisational intentions in relation to potential environmental effects.*

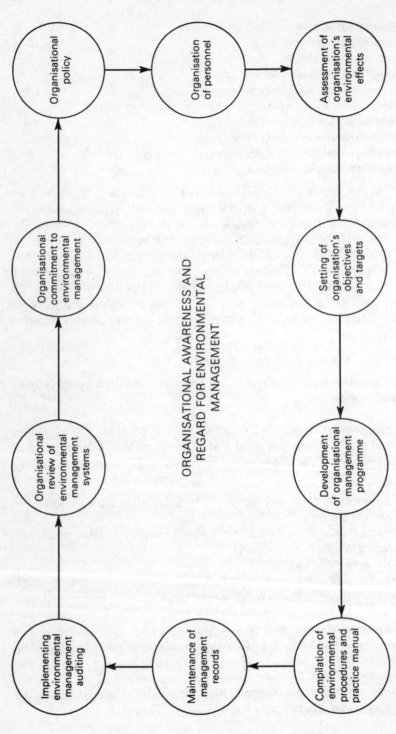

Figure 2.2 Structural overview of an organisation's environmental management system

Environmental Strategy
> *The organisation's considered actions in respect of its environmental situation in the formulation of policy, aims and objectives.*

Environmental Objectives
> *The measurable organisational targets, or goals, for environmental performance.*

Environmental Management Programme
> *The organisational approach to formalising the means of achieving environmental policy, aims and objectives.*

Environmental Management Manual
> *The organisation's documentation of procedures and working instructions for implementing the environmental management programme.*

Environmental Management Review
> *The management evaluation of its environmental system with regard to changing environmental awareness, conditions and legislation.*

Environmental Management Audit
> *The periodic detailed evolution of the organisation's environmental management system to determine its effectiveness in satisfying the environmental policy.*

2.4 Specific requirements of a system

The standard for environmental management systems specifies that an organisation should establish and maintain an environmental management system to ensure that its activities conform to its environmental policy, strategy, aims and objectives and meets current environmental legislation.

To achieve this, the following requirements must be met by an organisation and, moreover, be seen to be met:

- That a documented system of environmental procedures and working instructions (*environmental management manual*) exists within the organisation that meet the requirements of the Environmental Standard.
- That the environmental management procedures (*environmental management system*) are implemented in practice by the organisation.
- That the environmental management system is maintained and upgraded on an on-going basis (*environmental management reviews and environmental management audit*).

The achievement of these three requirements is essential to the internal development and use of an environmental management system but, moreover, they are most necessary in demonstrating to an external audience that the organisation is upholding its commitment to environmental issues. This is, of course, paramount when seeking wider recognition and certification for the organisation's environmental management system.

2.5   Environmental management system descriptors

BS 7750 sets out and describes the fundamental requirements for environmental management systems within a number of key sections, each presenting requirement descriptors. Again, attention is drawn to the Standard and the reader is directed to this for precise detail and description in compiling sections of a system to meet BS 7750 requirements.

Within the sections specified, each requirement is framed in terms of organisational responsibility around which the organisation can develop its system to suit its own range of activities. In this way the individuality and core business of the organisation can be accommodated. It does, of course, mean that an environmental management system is unique to that organisation and, therefore, a particular organisation may have need to develop some aspects to a greater or lesser extent based on their own perception of requirement. As an organisation works its way through the Standard it may have a need for guidance particular to its core activity and, therefore, it is essential that an organisation consults specialist sector guides relevant to its field of business. It may also seek additional authoritative guidance, for example that provided by a professional or regulatory body. Again, the reader is directed to the British Standards Institution (BSI) for further and more detailed information.

References

1   British Standards Institution (BSI), BS 7750: *Specification for Environmental Management Systems* (1992).
2   British Standards Institution (BSI), BS 5750: *Quality Systems* (1979, revised 1987).

3 Environmental Management: Detailed Requirements of a System

3.1 An environmental system

To clearly demonstrate that an organisation has concern for and commitment to environmental issues it must establish and maintain an environmental management system. This system shall ensure that the effects of an organisation's activities conform, first, with environmental legislation and, second, with its own stated environmental policy, objectives, principles and procedures.

The environmental management system should be a documented system of procedures and working instructions for practice and moreover the documented system must be seen to function effectively in implementation.

There is little doubt that any organisation will have some effect upon its environs and the environmental management system must effectively and efficiently provide measures for organisational interaction with its environment. Environmental management systems are complex in nature since they must address a multitude of influencing variables including not only the environmental aspect but the socio-technical characteristics of the organisation. Environmental management systems, therefore, require a comprehensive framework of structure, procedures and practices and necessitate a wealth of organisational skills, abilities and commitment.

Whilst some organisations may be, effectively, starting from scratch, other organisations may already have in place a management system suitable for modification to an environmental management system. BS 7750: Specification for Environmental Management Systems allows such sharing of organisational systems and resources. In such a situation, the Standard does expect the organisation to extend existing management systems providing the existing system itself is recognised, for example a BS 5750 quality system.

The environmental management system should be formulated and administered such that it fundamentally seeks to prevent adverse effects from organisational activity rather than retrospective detection and cure. It is therefore a pro-active organisational management system.

The priorities of an environmental management system should be to:

- Increase awareness of potential organisational effects upon the environment within the organisation.
- Take account of the specific environmental aspects interacting with the organisation and also broader environmental issues.
- Identify potential environmental effects arising from organisational activity.
- Meet current environmental legislation.
- Enable organisational priorities to be determined with a view to creating organisational policy, objectives and goals.
- Enable the planning, monitoring and control of organisational activity with regard to environmental effect.
- Facilitate auditing, review and update.
- Meet with criteria of external regulatory/registration bodies.
- Allow sufficient flexibility for change to meet future circumstances.

In order to meet these priorities an environmental management system should be developed with regard for those main system elements identified in Chapter 2, section 2.2 — Environmental Management System: Structure. This chapter considers the formulation of an environmental management system that will meet such a structure (see Figure 3.1).

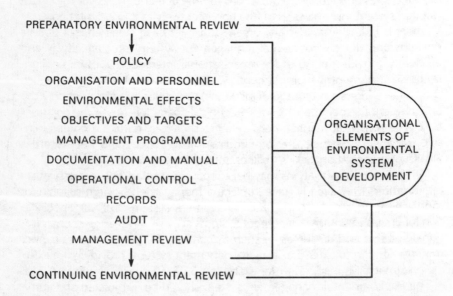

Figure 3.1 Elements of development for an environmental management system within an organisation

3.2   Preparatory environmental review

Definition

A preparatory environmental review is:

> the detailed consideration of all aspects of an organisation's business with regard to its environmental situation as a basis for developing an environmental management system

A preparatory environmental review is essential, particularly to an organisation with minimal or existing environmental management propensity, to determine the organisation's current environmental situation (see Figure 3.2). As defined, the purpose of the preparatory environmental review should be to determine the current environmental status of the organisation with a view to developing its environmental management system.

Key activities

In conducting a preparatory environmental review, the organisation should undertake the following key activities:

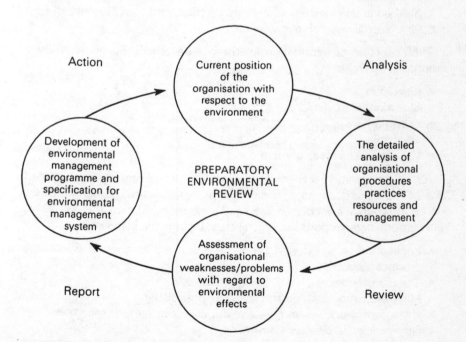

Figure 3.2   Organisational activity for preparatory environmental review

- A detailed examination of existing environmental management procedures and working practices.
- An evaluation of environmental effects resulting from organisational activities.
- Complete a register of the environmental effects of its business.
- Determine the principal legislative and regulatory requirements affecting the organisation's business and assess their requirements.
- Analyse organisational performance to identify areas of improvement.

Approach

To conduct a preparatory environmental review a combination of both qualitative and quantitative information will be required and whilst the methods will be determined by the characteristics of the organisation itself, basic approaches include the use of the following:

- Analysis of management structure and hierarchy.
- Divisional and departmental analysis of activity.
- Task analysis of activity.
- Longitudinal and cross sectional analysis of procedures and working instructions.
- Method and work study of working practices and use of resources.
- Operational research of procedures.

The collection of information for these aspects may be obtained by a number of methods:

- Checklists.
- Questionnaires.
- Consultations.
- Interviews.
- Inspection and measurement.

For an organisation with no formal environmental management system one of the initial steps to conducting a preparatory environmental review will be to produce a list of organisational areas for evaluation. This will, again, differ among organisations but typical areas include the following:

- Implication of the design processes upon environmental effect (e.g. product outputs).
- Use of resources.
- Minimisation of wastage and recycling possibilities.
- Hazardous processes and use and disposal of hazardous materials.
- Emergency and disaster assessment.
- Perceptual impact of the organisation upon the environment (visual, noise, and smell).

Preparatory environmental review report

Analysis and findings from the preparatory environmental review should be formalised in a report which should focus on three issues:

(i) The determination of the nature and extent of problems identified and the organisational priority and time frame for rectification measures.
(ii) The development of an environmental management programme of action to address the issues raised in (i) above and how this will be resourced and managed.
(iii) The required specification for the development of the organisation's environmental management system given its circumstances to address the aspects of (i) and (ii) above.

3.3   Formulation of policy

Definition

The Environmental Policy is

A published statement of organisational intentions in relation to potential environmental effects.

Organisational needs

Whilst the structure and content of an organisation's environmental policy will vary according to the needs of the organisation, any organisation must ask itself four basic questions (see Figure 3.3):

(i) What is the organisation's current environmental performance?
(ii) What is the organisation's envisaged future environmental performance?
(iii) What factors are assisting or preventing the organisation achieving its desired environmental performance?
(iv) What aspects of the organisation must be changed such that it may eclipse its desired environmental performance?

In asking these basic questions the organisation is not only setting out the basis for its environmental policy statement, but laying the foundations for its aims, objectives, strategies and procedures. Moreover, the need for organisational change will be addressed and certainly the issue of environmental management policy making is one which is sure to challenge long-established organisational attitudes, customs and procedures.

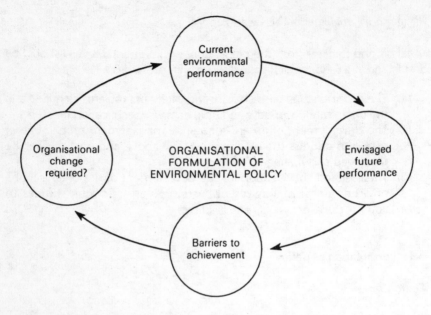

Figure 3.3   Organisational formulation of environmental policy: questions to be asked

An environmental management policy should:

- Define the organisation's corporate philosophy towards environmental management, in the context of its business activities.
- Be presented in the form of a policy statement, originating from the organisation's board of executive management.

Requirements

To be auspicious, an environmental policy must:

- Be relevant to the organisation's core activities.
- Assess, genuinely, the environmental effects of the organisation's activities.
- Be directed from executive level.
- Be implemented at all managerial levels within the organisation.
- Request commitment throughout the entire organisation and its workforce.
- Make provision for setting, implementing and maintaining the environmental performance of the organisation.
- Be available to regulatory bodies and, more widely, be available for public scrutiny.

Statement of policy

As the environmental policy statement is, essentially, the public face of an organisation's concern for and commitment to environmental issues, it should:

- Be clear and understandable and presented in simple format.
- Be a true reflection of organisational intention and principles for action with regard to potential environmental effects.
- Be linked to organisational aims, objectives and goals.
- Be published with corporate identity.
- Be flexible for use in organisational publicity material, i.e. the company's annual report, advertising products, etc.

In many organisations, the environmental policy will address a wide range of interests and intentions. The issues raised in the environmental policy will depend upon the nature of the organisation and, therefore, environmental policy will be as narrow or as broad as the organisation itself deems appropriate.

3.4 Organisation and personnel

Organisation and personnel aspects of environmental management systems are concerned with three key broad areas of consideration (see Figure 3.4). These are:

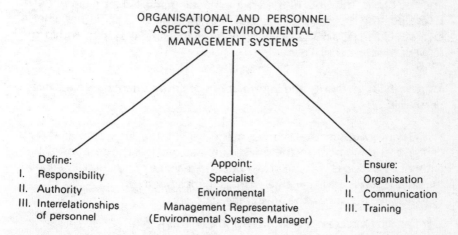

Figure 3.4   Requirement for organisation and personnel aspects in an organisation's environmental management system

(i)   Appointment of an environmental management representative.
(ii) Definition of responsibility, authority and interrelationships of environmental management personnel.
(iii) Organisation, communication and training of personnel involved with the environmental management system.

Environmental management representative

A management representative should be appointed by the organisation whose responsibility is for ensuring that the requirements of the environmental standard are met and the environmental management system is effectively implemented and maintained.

In an ideal situation, the management representative will assume responsibility exclusively for the organisation's environmental management system. It is more likely, however, that the management representative will assume responsibility for the environmental management system in addition to other organisational duties. In a larger organisation, an environmental management team may be constituted under the guidance of the assigned environmental management representative.

The role of the environmental management representative is to augment the traditional senior and middle management responsibilities and to co-ordinate environmental management activity throughout the organisation.

The environmental manager's remit extends to all aspects of the organisation's environmental management activity and therefore this covers the organisation's interrelationship with external organisations, regulatory bodies and the public. The work of the environmental management representative relies upon the support of all line-staff in all organisational disciplines who, in fact, should maintain the environmental management system within the remit of their responsibilities.

Responsibility, authority and interrelations of environmental management personnel

Within an environmental management system, the organisation should define and document in the environmental manual the responsibilities, authority and duties of those personnel who manage or functionally support the organisation's environmental management system.

To achieve the above, the organisation should:

- Provide all necessary resources to sustain the system.
- Clearly assign personnel to system duties.
- Promote action to ensure compliance with the organisation's environmental policy.

- Identify organisational problems and initiate action in response.
- Ensure the capability to monitor, control, review and audit the system.
- Assign personnel to function in an emergency or disaster situation.

Organisation, communication and training

Within the general company organisation, management should determine the capabilities, skills, qualifications and experience of those persons who may be assigned to the environmental management system to ensure they can meet the explicit demands of the system. Organisation for the environmental management system should be arranged around such skilled and experienced personnel assigned to duties within the typical hierarchical framework of senior, middle and lower management. Where appropriate, job descriptions should reflect environmental management duties and performance criteria.

Good communication is essential to any organisation and to any organisational aspect and it is also crucial to the development of the environmental management system. Communication through the organisational hierarchy should follow the usual good practices of short, succinct lines of communications allowing open and effective feedback routes which are essential to environmental management review and auditing.

Training

As environmental management may be a new departure for many organisations, training and education may need to be provided. This is needed for personnel at all levels of the organisation, as follows:

- For senior and executive management to ensure they understand the basis of an environmental management system such that they can generate policy, aims and objectives.
- For middle management to ensure they have sufficient training to develop and implement the environmental management system.
- For junior level staff and personnel to ensure they can operate the environmental management system in practice.
- For new personnel to ensure that despite turnover of staff the system can be maintained.
- For existing personnel to ensure training up-dates accommodate new initiatives or changing circumstances.

These requirements for training may be accommodated by the organisation in the following ways:

- Open participation in environmental initiatives.
- Introducing training programmes.
- Regular Continuing Professional Development (CPD) courses.
- In house, on-site open learning experiences.

Such training initiatives will allow the organisation to ensure that:

- Management and the workforce will have greater awareness for and appreciation of environmental issues within their organisation.
- Personnel will see the potential consequences of departure from good environmental management system practices and will be able to respond accordingly.

3.5   Environmental Effects

Definition

> *The effects of organisational activity upon its environs whether direct or indirect, detrimental or beneficial.*

Evaluation of environmental effects

Within an environmental management system, the organisation should develop, implement and monitor procedures for examining and evaluating the effects of its organisational activity upon the environment. As determined in Chapter 1, such environmental effects may be direct or indirect, be adverse or beneficial or be unclear or manifest.

Classification of environmental effects by an organisation may include the following (see Figure 3.5):

- Emissions to the atmosphere.
- Discharges to water.
- Expulsion of solid, liquid and other wastes.
- Use of land and natural resources.
- Emission of other pollutants – noise, odour, dust.
- Visual or comfort disturbances.
- Contamination of land and other resources.
- Damage to balance of eco-system structures.

Any of the aforementioned environmental effects may occur due to one of the following acts.

- The normal business and operating procedures of the organisation.
- Business or operating procedures outside the usual or normal parameters of the organisation.
- Accidents or catastrophe.

The level of detail of an environmental effects evaluation will depend upon a number of specific issues:

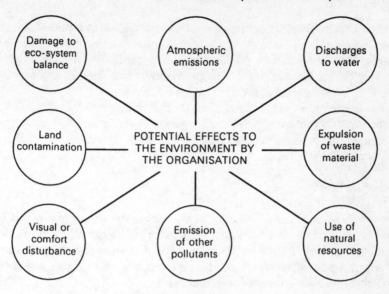

Figure 3.5　Some of the major environmental effects of organisational activity

- The legislative requirements relating to the particular environmental effect and the relative situation of the organisation to these requirements.
- The nature and range of the organisation's activity and its environmental policy towards this activity.
- The knowledge base within the organisation to determine and evaluate the above.

Most organisations should pay heed to legislative and regulatory requirements in conducting their environmental effects evaluation. Particular attention is drawn to authoritative guidance and sector codes of practice which may influence organisational activity prohibitively.

In evaluating environmental effects, it is essential to determine the effect not only during normal operating conditions but to anticipate the likely effect to the environment of abnormal activity, accident or catastrophe. Risk assessment may be used to evaluate the potential degree of danger from the above situation and depending upon the priorities determined, potential actions to mitigate effects can be considered.

Evaluation of the environmental effects of third party activities

In addition to the activities of the organisation itself, the activities of third parties (suppliers and services) should be evaluated for potential environmental effect. Whilst some suppliers or service organisations may have their own environmental management systems, ensuring some degree of environmental friendliness in their products or services, many do not. Although it is unlikely that a full evaluation can be made in this respect, the procuring organisation should do all it can to assess this aspect.

The organisation should also consider the environmental efficacy of any company it subsumes within its own organisation on acquisition or merger to ensure it inherits responsibilities that meet with its own environmental philosophy and commitment.

Future activity

The organisation should evaluate the environmental effects of any potential new or innovative processes or practices or modification to be made to working practices. This is essential to ensuring that any potential environmental effects are considered at the earliest opportunity. All information relating to the environmental effects of the business are documented in a Register of Environmental Effects, a requirement of BS 7750.

Evaluation of legislative, regulatory and other control mechanisms

As an integral part of the environmental effects evaluation, the organisation should establish appropriate procedures to monitor and record changing legislation, regulatory and other control requirements relevant to the functioning of the organisation and to the potential effects of the organisation upon the environment. This evaluation is documented in the organisation's Register of Regulations, again a requirement under BS 7750.

3.6   Environmental aims and objectives

Definition

Environmental objectives are:

> The measurable organisational targets or goals for environmental performance.

An organisation must establish and maintain procedures to specify its objectives and measurable goals or targets at each management level within the organisation.

The objectives developed and goals set must be directed towards conforming to the stated environmental policy and since they must measure performance achieved against an environmental plan they should relate environmental performance to a set time-frame (see Figure 3.6).

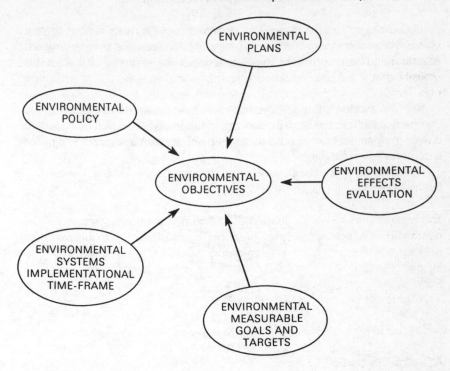

Figure 3.6   The determinants of environmental objectives within an organisation

Because environmental management systems are pro-active in nature and dynamic in their evolution, the objectives should demonstrate organisational commitment to continual improvement and development. Aims and objectives should be determined with due reference to the environmental effects evaluation and quantified where this is feasible for the development of performance goals or targets. Goals and targets set should be quantifiable and must be realistic and achievable and related to the activities of those managers and personnel responsible for particular aspects of the environmental management system.

3.7   Management programme

Definition

The Environmental Management programme is:

the organisational approach to formalising the means of achieving environmental policy, aims and objectives.

As part of any environmental management system, an organisation must establish and maintain an environmental management programme (see Figure 3.7). The programme must describe three essential characteristics, these being:

(i)   The assignment of responsibility for environmental management functions within the organisation at various levels.
(ii) A specification of goals or targets for performance at the different levels of management.
(iii) The way in which environmental management is to be achieved.

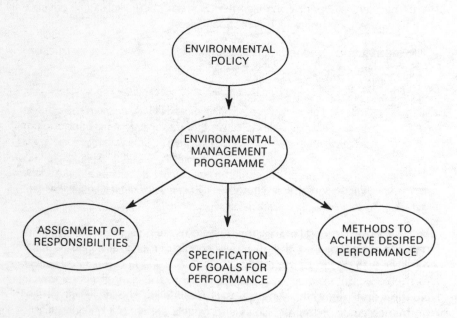

Figure 3.7   The key areas of the environmental management programme for environmental system development

Any programme should identify and specify the following:

• The environmental objectives that are to be achieved.
• The means for achieving these objectives.
• The mechanisms for managing changing circumstances as encountered in implementation.
• The corrective actions needed should difficulties arise in implementation.

The environmental management programme is fundamental to the development of the environmental management system as it is the core mechanism transferring organisational environmental policy into procedures and working practices. The importance of this management aspect of system development is expanded in Chapter 4.

3.8   Environmental management documentation

Definition

The primary environmental management system document is the environmental management manual. This manual represents:

> *The organisation's documentation of procedures and working instructions for implementing the environmental management programme.*

The manual serves as an organisation's reference point for implementation and maintenance of the environmental management system. In its simplest format, the manual can be likened to a organisation's general handbook of rules and working procedures but explicitly directed towards environmental management.

The nature of environmental management documentation can take many forms depending upon the organisation's business and circumstances but generally follows a collection of written works:

(i)   An environmental management system manual encompassing the whole organisation.

(ii)   Supplementary manuals encompassing departmental or divisional activity within the organisation.

(iii)   Specialist manuals encompassing specific organisational tasks and functions.

Whilst the precise nature, format and content of the environmental management manual will differ amongst organisations the general sections forming the structure of the manual should be as follows:

- Contents list.
- Revision list.
- Distribution list.
- Statement of authorisation.
- Summary and instructions for use.
- Policy description.
- Organisational structure.
- Applicable standards and regulations.

- Aims and objectives.
- Programme and procedures.
- Goals and targets.
- Operation and control mechanisms.
- Record systems.
- Review and auditing.
- Training.
- Application to 'third party' (sub-contract) organisations.

Each of the main headings listed above may be subdivided into further levels of detailing of system specification. This format therefore follows quite closely the basic format of a BS 5750: quality system, which many organisations will already be familiar with.

3.9   Operational control

Operational control within an environmental management system encompasses three organisational aspects:

(i)   Control mechanisms.
(ii) Verification, measurement and testing.
(iii) Non-compliance and corrective action.

Control

The organisation should identify activities which hold propensity to affect the environment relevant to the organisation's policy and objectives. The organisation should plan and carry out such activities to ensure that they are conducted under controlled conditions. Control of organisational activity should consider:

- Procedures and working instructions contained within the organisation's environmental management manual.
- Criteria for environmental performance of the procedures and instructions.
- Monitoring and recording of activities within procedures.
- Procedures for managing 'third party' (sub-contract) organisations.

Verification, measurement and testing

The environmental management system should develop and maintain verification procedures to ensure that organisational practices meet with the specification propounded in the environmental programme. Verification should be undertaken by system area, or specific activities, and, for each, the following tasks are pertinent:

- Specify the verification information needed from the system.
- Specify the verification procedures.
- Specify performance levels expected to achieve verified practices.
- Specify action to be taken if deficiency is identified during verification.
- Specify that complete documentation is prerequisite.

The nature, scope and detail of verification procedures should be contingent to the importance of the organisational aspect they review.

Although it is not always possible, verification should be a measurable activity where actual performance can be assessed by measurement or testing. In such cases the following should be undertaken:

- Specify the measurement to be undertaken.
- Specify the procedures to be used.
- Specify acceptable performance.
- Define the accuracy of the expected results.
- Specify the recording mechanisms to be utilised.

Non-compliance and corrective action

The environmental management system should develop and maintain procedures for analysing activities which do not conform with the performance expected (see Figure 3.8). For such instances, the environmental management representative or management team should:

- Investigate the aspect suspected of non-conformance.
- Determine the problem, its nature and extent.
- Identify the cause of the difficulty.
- Consider action to remedy the situation.
- Initiate action.
- Monitor and record attempts to rectify.
- Adopt improved procedures.
- Document revised procedures.

Structured investigation of suspected non-conformance in this way will allow the environmental management system to respond to deficient procedures and working practices in the most efficient and effective way and check system problems at an early stage to avoid prolonged detrimental environmental effects occurring.

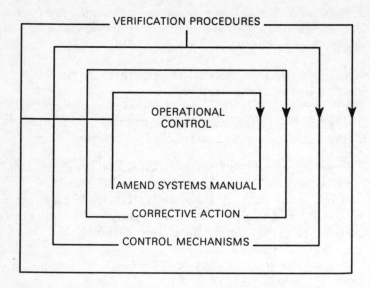

Figure 3.8   Operational control mechanisms within the environmental management system

3.10   Maintaining records

The organisation should develop and maintain a formalised set of environmental management system records. This is essential in demonstrating compliance with the system and also to facilitate evaluation of performance. Environmental management system records should be maintained for all system aspects and should be stored such that they can be easily retrieved for use within the on-going system or to provide information for auditing and review purposes. The records system should be a composite part of the environmental management documentation, that is, it should be described within the environmental manual.

The organisation should develop a records system in which records are:

- Maintained for all organisational system aspects.
- Identifiable to activities.
- Indexed.
- Filed systematically.
- Stored appropriately.
- Maintained and updated.
- Available for internal and external use.

3.11 Audit

Definition

Environmental management audits are:

The periodic detailed evaluation of the organisation's environmental management system to determine its effectiveness in satisfying the environmental policy.

An environmental management system should develop and maintain appropriate procedures for conducting audits. Auditing may be internal for use in on-going review of the system or can be external for environmental assessment audits or certification purposes.

Auditing is essential to determine:

- That the environmental management system is following the organisation's management programme and is being implemented correctly.
- That the environmental management system is fulfilling those requirements specified by the organisation's environmental policy.

To implement auditing effectively, the organisation should develop an audit plan. The audit plan is a systematic approach to determining the organisational aspects to be audited, frequency of auditing, procedures to be used, persons responsible, and method of reporting.

Environmental audits may be carried out internally by organisational personnel but to achieve impartial assessment external auditors may be employed. In addition, audits may be conducted by external control agencies, for example certification bodies and regulatory organisations.

Auditing should be the responsibility of the environmental management representative who should initiate the audit, monitor its progress, collate information for analysis and distribute reports to all organisational levels, and when external auditors or other parties are involved, co-ordinate their activities.

Auditing is a crucial environmental management system activity and, therefore, it is paramount that the organisation conducts audits with efficacy and to a recognised procedure. Organisations may, in addition to obtaining auditing guidance from BS 7750,[1] consult more specialist guidance given in BS 5750: Quality Systems[2] and BS 7229: Guide to Quality Systems Auditing.[3]

3.12 Management reviews

An essential aspect of the environmental management system is periodic management review. The organisation should ensure that management review of the system is conducted at appropriate intervals to, first, monitor the system and, second, to ensure the system continues to meet with requirements of the Standard and current legislation.

The nature and extent of the environmental management review should encompass the entire organisation and all activities. Such review is the responsibility of the environmental management representative who may assign internal personnel or external reviewers.

Management review should always follow environmental management system audits and should ensure that:

- Existing systems meet the current organisation's operational requirements.
- Any changes to legislation are incorporated within revised policy, objectives and procedures.
- All recommendations made in the audit have been implemented.
- The present system meets all prevailing circumstances in the wider context of organisational activity.

Environmental management review should form an integral part of system development and therefore should be documented like all other environmental management system aspects.

3.13   Continuing environmental review

Because environmental management systems are a pro-active and dynamic management activity, the system is not simply complete once the eleven key organisational elements of environmental systems development have been satisfied. In fact, at this stage the environmental management system is merely up and running. The system has to be monitored, reviewed and upgraded as organisational experience is acquired. The environmental management system therefore must be regarded as an evolving organisational concept and be subject to continuing environmental review.

The importance of continuing environmental review is not merely the maintenance of the system but the broader issues of environmental management across the organisation and in relation to the environmental situation the organisation continues to find itself in. Change is an occupational hazard of almost all organisations. The organisation must not only keep itself abreast of the current situation within the organisation but continuously monitor and appraise outside influences, such as the changing environment, legislation, regulation, economic, political and market orientated forces to ensure the organisation's environmental management system continues to meet current demands.

For these reasons continuing environmental review must be formalised as an 'overview' mechanism supplementing the management review of the system outlined in section 3.12. The substance of the continual review should also be formally discussed, analysed and actions considered at least annually and at other times where deemed necessary, to respond to changing circumstances.

Reviews of this type, addressing the broader issues of environmental management may well precede the organisation's annual report; in fact, information generated in the continuing review may well form an important part of organisational reports to commerce, industry and the public. Continuing environmental review can therefore represent an important organisational mechanism in the public face of environmental management. This aspect is discussed further in Chapter 4: Developing an Environmental Management System within the Organisation.

References

1   British Standards Institution (BSI), BS 7750: *Specification for Environmental Management Systems* (1992).
2   British Standards Institution (BSI), BS 5750: *Quality Systems* (1979, revised 1987).
3   British Standards Institution (BSI), BS 7229: *Guide to Quality Systems Auditing, (Part 1), Qualification Criteria for Auditors (Part 2), Managing an Audit Programme (Part 3)* (all 1991).

4 Developing an Environmental Management System within the Organisation

4.1 Rationale and conceptual approach

An environmental management system aims to provide a platform on which the organisation can best meet its responsibilities to, and show commitment for, the environment. It forms the basis upon which improvements to the organisation can be founded and, moreover, it portrays to the outside world that the organisation's business is conducted with consistency to a standard that is recognised and respected.

Any organisation, where control of its activities is essentially weak, will undoubtedly encounter difficulties. As problems set in, business can go awry, profitability can diminish and commercial markets can dwindle. An environmental management system, like most all management systems, presents structure, clarity and focus to organisational activity such that the many problems that could occur do not, as the system self-perpetuates and guides the organisation, with appropriate management.

An environmental management system is unequivocally useful to an organisation because it is not merely introspective, like so many systems, but looks beyond the organisational boundaries. It allows the organisation to see itself in the wider context and to take store of its whole manifestation.

To an organisation that already has extensive management systems in place, developing an environmental management system should pose few problems. For an organisation that does not, considerable thought must be given to the formulation and development of an environmental management system if is to be implemented with efficacy.

Environmental management: questions the organisation should ask

An organisation must ask itself three fundamental questions:

(i) Why does the organisation need an environmental management system?
(ii) How does it develop an environmental management system?
(iii) What does the organisation seek to achieve through an environmental management system?

(i) Why does the organisation need an environmental management system?

If an organisation is so fortunate that its position in the commercial market-place is not governed at all by environmentally driven market forces then that organisation may have little need, if any, to adopt an environmental management stance. Almost all organisations, however, are influenced by environmental factors and issues and must take cognisance of their demands in the constitution of their organisation and business activities. A number of key reasons present a compelling argument for the adoption of an environmental management system. These are:

- *Perception*
  Organisations in most commercial sectors are increasingly concerned with achieving and demonstrating better environmental performance as wider attitudes, economic and other pressures seek to encourage environmental protection.
- *Legislation*
  Organisations are becoming greatly aware of increasingly stringent legislation for environmental performance at local, national and international levels.
- *Regulation*
  Organisations perceive the increasing trend in many commercial sectors for environmental assessments, reviews or audits focusing upon the organisation's business, sector operation, or project specific activity.
- *Business*
  Organisations are more aware of the need to take account of the environmental effects of their business within their management processes to be better placed to obviate potential liability resulting from inadequate practices or defective outputs. They realise that an environmental management framework should negate the likelihood of such occurrences. In addition, it is recognised that an organisation which adopts formal environmental management will be better placed to meet the increasing trend towards pre-qualification criteria specified by clients, particularly within public sector procurement. It is recognised that an organisation which demonstrates commitment to environmentally sound business practice should find itself more competitive and better accepted in the commercial marketplace than an organisation that takes no account of environmental management.
- *Recognition*
  Organisations are realising that there will be the need not only to pursue an environmental management philosophy but, moreover, to demonstrate to the outside world that organisational activity complies with a unified and recognised national and international environmental standard.

- *Organisation*
  Organisations understand that their business performance is heavily dependent upon the quality of the human resource and the methods by which this is structured and organised. They are also aware that a structured framework of environmental management is essential in meeting organisational efficiency and effectiveness. An environmental management system is able to address all of the aforementioned organisational concerns.

(ii) How does the organisation develop an environmental management system?

Before developing a systems approach to environmental management, an organisation may choose to consider the options available to it. In fact, an organisation only has one alternative to the environmental management system, an *inspection approach*.

Inspection approach

The organisation can continue with its existing management and organisational practices and improve supervision and inspection procedures to accommodate environmental management in specific organisational activities. (This may be all that is required in a small organisation or one with very limited environmental effects from its business.)

Many organisations develop control mechanisms in this way, and whilst in some organisations increased supervision and inspection can raise performance acceptably there are a number of distinct disadvantages:

- Most organisations are sufficiently complex that all activities cannot be managed in this way.
- Inspection is, essentially, retrospective in nature and does not present any propensity towards 'preventive' environmental management.
- The cost of remedial action for organisational and management deficiency following inspection greatly exceeds the cost of 'getting it right first time'.
- Increased supervision and inspection is, over the longer term, a cost-prohibitive management activity.

For these reasons, an organisation seeking to adopt environmental management must, realistically, develop an environmental management system.

Systems approach

The organisation can develop an environmental management ethos through the formulation and implementation of a management system to incorporate *all* aspects of organisational activity. Such an approach aims to provide procedures and methods of working that either prevent problems arising or identify and manage problems in the most efficient and cost effective way.

A systems approach is especially applicable because:

- It is a 'whole organisation' philosophy and concept and environmental management must be applied across organisational activity; it cannot be applied to organisational aspects in isolation.
- It is a formally structured management approach to developing uniform organisational procedures to meet desired environmental performance.
- It presents a well-defined framework that structures organisational resources to meet the demands of environmental management in the most cost-effective way.
- It is a pro-active rather than retrospective solution that is essentially preventive, but quickly reactive, in nature and can meet the dynamic characteristics required of environmental management.

(iii) What does the organisation seek to achieve through an environmental management system?

The organisation must decide what it is that it seeks to control or manage and against what criteria its performance will be judged. In the context of an environmental management system the organisation is seeking to develop:

an organisational framework, structure, procedure and practice for implementing environmental management to stated policy and objectives.

Performance will be measured against stated goals and targets and to those criteria specified by applicable standards and current legislation. The system will be documented and amenable to review and audit in accordance with good systems practice.

The organisation must appraise these aspects in the light of organisational characteristics and circumstance and the likely effect of organisational activity upon its environs. An environmental management system can be as narrow or as broad as the situation demands. A systems approach is therefore applicable to most organisations. Guidance for environmental management system development is presented in BS 7750: Specification for Environmental Management Systems.[1]

The essence of any system of this type may, in simple terms, be described as:

- saying what the organisation does.
- doing what the organisation says.
- recording that it has been done.

Adopting a systems approach

Before developing an environmental management system, an organisation will need to consider the implications of a systems philosophy upon the organisation in several important areas.

- The core business of the organisation and the effects on its environment.
- The level of system required given organisational characteristics and circumstances.
- The development time, cost and systems quality required to meet organisational needs.
- The advantages and disadvantages of a systems approach to the organisation.

Core business

As an environmental management system is the public face of organisational activity, it must be seen as a realistic reflection of intent and commitment to the environment, based around the core business of the organisation. It must aim to mitigate and, moreover, be seen to mitigate the most central and vital potential effects upon the environment of the organisation. Anything less than this will hold little respect with those outside the organisation. The environmental management system, therefore, must be structured around the core business and encompass all organisational activities, not merely fringe elements.

Level of system

An environmental management system should be structured predominantly to meet the needs of the organisation. All organisations are different and therefore require an environmental management system with a level of detail that describes accurately its own organisational characteristics and environmental situations.

Development time, cost and system quality

Like most aspects of organisation, an environmental management system will require considerable development time and incur relatively high development costs. These two important factors are unavoidable, and are balanced finely, and are also counterbalanced themselves by a third factor, that of desired system quality. Any imbalance in one of these factors will have a corresponding effect upon the other two. Any organisation will undoubtedly be seeking a 'best-buy' environmental management system, one that gives the best overall performance and system quality for the cost expended and the time devoted to development, implementation and maintenance. In the absence of cost–benefit analysis in environmental systems development, the most equitable balance of factors cannot be accurately determined. An organisation should, however, take a lead from quality systems development where implementing a quality assurance system is frequently seen as simply good for business, maximising turnover and profit in the longer term at the expense of the short-term development burdens.

Advantages and Disadvantages of a Systems Approach
The recognised advantages of using a systems approach are as follows:

- Identified framework and structure.
- Uniform procedures and practices.
- Documented evidence of compliance to performance criteria.
- Improved communications and interdisciplinary efficiency.
- Inherent preventive and reactive management capability.
- More rapid response to organisational problems or difficulty.
- Effective accommodation of situational and organisational change.
- Improved commercial competitiveness and marketability.
- External recognition of organisational compliance to agreed system standards.

The accepted disadvantages of adopting a systems approach include:

- High developmental costs (in particular where an organisation is starting from scratch).
- Increased staffing requirements (will further increase developmental costs either in acquiring new staff or training existing staff).
- Excessive paperwork generation. (It is generally regarded that a systems approach perpetuates bureaucracy through copious documentation. Certainly there will be some additional paperwork, or other medium of record keeping, but this need not necessarily be excessively bureaucratic.)

Again, experience in quality assurance systems has shown, quite unequivocally, that such disadvantages to adopting a systems approach are likely to be outweighed by the longer- term benefits enjoyed by the organisation.

Once an organisation has considered its general rationale and conceptual approach to environmental management, it can progress to develop an environmental management system within the organisation. The first step is to conduct a *preparatory environmental review*.

4.2   The organisation's preparatory environmental review

The organisational benchmark

Preparatory environmental review begins with an organisation asking itself a number of fundamental questions. These questions and the answers that are postulated form the organisation's reference point or benchmark from which an environmental management system can be developed.

- Where is the organisation now?
- Where does the organisation wish to go?
- Why is the organisation going?
- How does the organisation get there?
- What will be achieved when the organisation gets there?

The process of developing and implementing an environmental management system will, subsequent to the consideration of the aforementioned questions, follow a set of definite stages. These are:

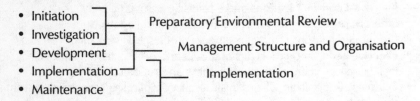

- Initiation　　　⎤
- Investigation　⎦　　　Preparatory Environmental Review
- Development　　　　　　Management Structure and Organisation
- Implementation　　⎤　　　Implementation
- Maintenance　　　　⎦

These stages, representing a dynamic systems process of organisational thinking, management structuring, organisational proceduring and implementation will quite naturally overlap as indicated. See Figure 4.12 later in this chapter for an overall schematic view of an environmental management system structure.

Initiation

Environmental management system development begins with the initiation stage and the organisation's perceived need for environmental management to meet both internal and external business activity. As seen in the preceding section in this chapter, an organisation really has little choice but to develop a systems approach since the only alternative is to increase supervision and adopt an inspection approach, which is seen to be cost-prohibitive and inadequate for all but the basic organisational demands. Once executive management has taken the decision to adopt an environmental management system within the organisation, the process of development proceeds to the investigation stage. It is taken as axiomatic that the organisation has both the perceived need and commitment to the environmental effects of its business to bring it this far in the thinking process.

Appointment of an environmental manager*

(* BS 7750 refers to the appointment of an Environmental Management Representative)

Although consideration of the organisational management structure to handle the environmental management system is an aspect of the Development stage and will follow subsequently, executive management may choose to appoint an existing or new senior member of staff in the role of Environmental Manager during the initiation stage. The role, duties and responsibilities of the environmental manager were briefly mentioned in Chapter 3 and are developed later in this chapter.

The required steps in the organisational thinking process for the Initiation stage are reflected in Figure 4.1 which can be related to the total system framework shown in Figure 4.12.

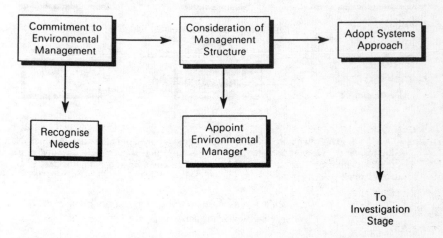

*BS 7750 specifies the appointment of an Environmental Management Representative

Figure 4.1   The initiation stage of environmental management system development and implementation

Investigation

The first and second steps in the Investigation stage are to establish the current position of the organisation in relation to environmental management (see Figure 4.2). This involves two distinct aspects:

(i)   Analysis of the existing organisation (*the internal view*)
(ii) Environmental review (*the external view*)

Analysis of the existing organisation

This aspect of the development process is essential to the future success of the environmental management system. The system must be developed as part of the existing organisational management procedures and formulated

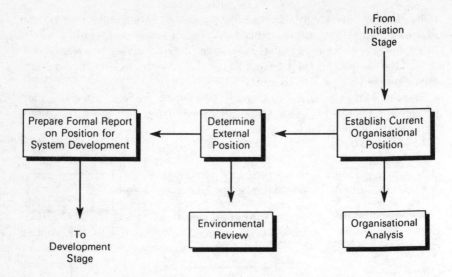

Note: Although preparatory environmental review in the organisational sense subsumes the initiation and investigation stages, in the structure shown this activity node represents the organisation's formal review of its environs and demands placed by its environs

Figure 4.2   The investigation stage of environmental management systems development and implementation

around the core activity of the business. It is fundamental, therefore, that management should analyse in detail the existing organisation to establish its current propensity for environmental management and to identify where change and improvements to organisation and procedures might be effected to best serve the environmental management system.

Analysing the existing organisation may, to some, appear somewhat unnecessary, a burden, even a threat. It is essential that management overcome any disbeliefs, anxiety and scepticism at this stage as the process of review paves the way for a systems approach where constant review is inherent and significant. Almost always, analysis of the existing organisation will represent a process of improvement and handled tactfully will allow management and the workforce to find for themselves better procedures and working practices.

There are a number of methods which can be successfully used to effect analysis. These are:

- Self analysis – conducted by department or section.
- Organisational 'in-house' analysis – conducted by the environmental management team.
- External analysis – conducted by external consultants.

In all cases, investigation and analysis should be co-ordinated by the environmental manager or the environmental management team.

Information for analysis may be acquired using the following methods:

- Study of existing procedures, with reference to the organisation's handbook of operating procedures and practices.
- Task analysis of specific organisational activity relevant to the future system development.
- Review of documentary evidence highlighting what has happened within the organisation.
- Structured interviews with relevant personnel.
- Detailed questionnaires to key and routine personnel.

It is essential that the information obtained is gathered from all organisational departments, sections and activities to provide the most complete documentation available on how the organisation has been run in the past and how it is currently operating. This is vital to establishing the organisation's internal benchmark.

Environmental review

The aim of the environmental review is to focus upon the external position such that the organisation can consider all aspects of its business, to identify its strengths and weaknesses, opportunities and risks, the effects of its business upon the environment and the implications of external forces upon the functioning of the organisation.

The review should encompass four key areas:

(i) Examination of all existing environmental management procedures and practices (if any).
(ii) Evaluation of significant environmental effects of the organisation's business.
(iii) Assessment of environmental infringements (or likelihood of potential future infringements).
(iv) Requirements of legislation and regulating bodies.

The organisational areas to which the above investigation might be directed is determined by the organisation given its own individual characteristics, situation and remit of business. Generally, however, environmental review should always:

- Identify problems and determine their extent and cause.
- Determine action needed to rectify such problems.

Information from these two aspects can then be fed into the formal report on systems development.

Report on organisational position for systems development

This report should be a formal digest on the current position of the organisation with respect to environmental management practices and the development of an environmental management system. It should be conclusive, based upon balanced and objective evaluation of all information generated and, in addition, it should incorporate facts and opinions expressed by management and staff.

The report should comment on the following:

- The organisation's present framework, structure and organisation.
- The organisation's current management philosophy.
- The organisation's procedures and practices.
- The roles, duties and responsibilities of sections, departments and personnel.
- The problems and difficulties identified by the organisation in its current practice.
- The change or modifications needed within the organisation to effect improvements.
- The proposed outline programme for developing the environmental management system.

Once an organisation has successfully undertaken a preparatory environmental review it can look ahead to the three very intensive stages of environmental management system creation, Development, Implementation and Maintenance. An organisation can view the systems analysis of these aspects under two broad headings:

(i)   Management Structure and Organisation.
(ii) Implementation.

4.3   Management structure and organisation

Development stage

The Development Stage of environmental management systems creation should satisfy the requirements of the following elements:

- Environmental policy.
- Environmental effects.
- Organisation and personnel.*
- Environmental objectives and targets.
- Environmental management programme.
- Environmental management manual and documentation.*

* For these system elements there will be some overlap with the Implementation Stage (see Figure 4.3).

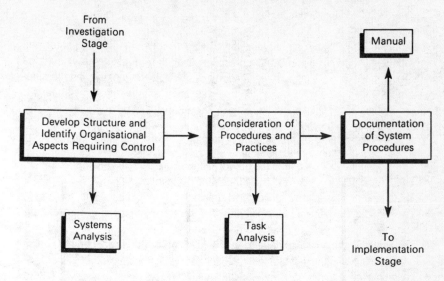

Figure 4.3   The development stage of environmental management systems

Management structure and organisation for environmental management systems

Management structure

A general management structure for an environmental system follows much the same pattern as management for other systems implementation. Three levels of management are applicable, these being:

(i)   Strategic.
(ii) Directive.
(iii) Operational.

Figure 4.4 presents a schematic management approach to environmental systems development within an organisation.

Strategic

The strategic level of management focuses upon the remit of the organisation's board of directors and executive management whose primary function is to sanction system development and provide executive organisational leadership in the following aspects of the environmental system:

• Environmental policy.
• Environmental statement.
• Aims and objectives.
• Goal and target setting.

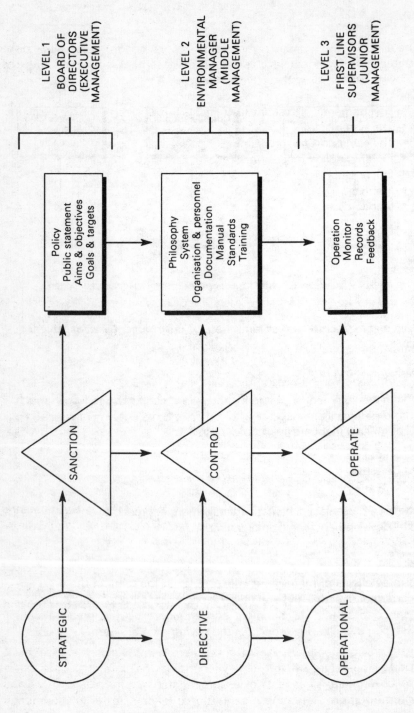

Figure 4.4   Management approach to environmental systems development within an organisation

Directive

The directive level of management focuses upon control. Responsible to the strategic management level, directive management is charged with the following aspects of system development:

- Environmental philosophy (as it affects the running of the organisation).
- The system itself.
- The environmental programme.
- Organisation and personnel.
- Documentation.
- Manuals.
- Standards.
- Training.

Operational

The operational level of management focuses upon the activities of first-line supervisors who operate or implement the environmental management system on a day-to-day basis. Responsible to directive level, operational management is responsible for the following aspects:

- Operation of the system.
- Monitoring.
- Record keeping.
- Provision of feedback.

Co-ordinating role of the environmental manager

It was identified in section 4.2 that an important aspect of environmental systems development is the appointment by the organisation of an environmental manager. BS 7750[1] specifies that:

The organisation shall appoint a management representative who, irrespective of other responsibilities, shall have defined authority and responsibility for ensuring that the requirements of this standard are implemented and maintained.

The environmental manager is a key person in the system development structure (see Figure 4.5). The primary function of the environmental manager is to co-ordinate *all* aspects of environmental systems development and implementation. Assuming organisational leadership for environmental management, this position is an integral part of directive level management, responsible for operational management, and accountable to strategic management. This senior position is expected to be commensurate with senior managers of organisational divisions or departments – in fact those who also function at the directive organisational level.

Organisation

A general organisational structure for an environmental management system is illustrated in Figure 4.5. Organisation essentially follows any normal hierarchical command structure with the addition of the specific appointment of the environmental manager. Assuming that the organisation follows a departmental, divisional or sectional dissipation of activities, each group of activity, purchasing, production, and so on, will be led by section supervisors at operational management level supported by heads of directive management level. This structure will provide the shortest and clearly defined routes of authority, responsibility, communication and feedback within the organisation.

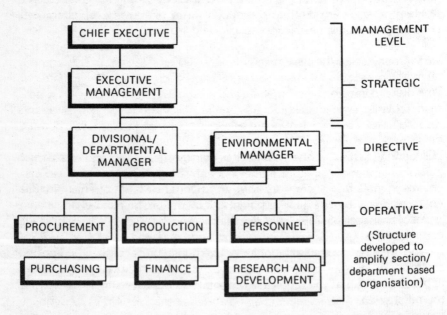

* Functioned by the first line system supervisors (junior management) in each department

Figure 4.5   Organisational management structure for environmental management system

Systems development: the functions of strategic management

(i) Environmental policy

Policy formulation is fundamental to the development of an organisation's environmental management system since it forms the basis for creating the environmental management programme, the operational elements within the programme and the assignment of responsibilities to management and the workforce. To assist managerial leadership and motivation of employees the policy must be clearly determined at the strategic management level and filtered down through each level of the managerial hierarchy through practical and understandable procedures and working instructions. This is, of course, achieved through the implementation of the environmental management manual, in effect a company handbook of procedures relating to environmental management as it affects the organisation.

At the institutional level, policy must, in practice, be sufficiently flexible to accommodate change in organisational circumstance or in response to changes in environmental situation or developing legislation. At an implementation level, like all managerial policies, the environmental management policy must be sufficiently rigid to promote any necessary change to current working practices within the organisation whilst making the workforce feel comfortable with any such change.

It is essential that a clear policy emerges in the eyes of staff and the workforce since day-to-day organisational activities in respect of environmental management are, like many other managerial concepts, often a matter of employee attitude, respect, integrity and personal desire for high work performance. Whilst environmental management policy should be exclusively the responsibility of executive or board level management, its development must be such that each level of management and workforce can relate to its philosophy. In this way, the policy will become a meaningful and established part of organisational culture, framework and structure. Only in this way can environmental management be developed and fostered throughout the entire organisation, this being essential to its successful realisation.

Policy must reflect 'top-down' management with the biggest commitment coming from strategic management, ably assisted by the designated environmental manager. It is their fundamental support for and commitment to environmental issues that must pervade the entire organisation. In systems application it is nearly always a fundamental lack of policy and direction from the most senior management in an organisation that leads to its subsequent failure in implementation.

The issues raised in the formulation of policy will depend upon the individual nature of the organisation. Whilst environmental policy in smaller organisations may be quite specific yet narrow in scope and extent, in a larger organisation environmental policy can cover a broad range of organisational activities and encompass many employees.

Organisational environmental policy may show commitment to, for example:

* Minimising or eliminating pollutive substances.
* Reducing organisational waste.
* Reducing energy consumption.
* Using environmentally sound resources.

Overall policy may then be further described for intra-organisational clarification on specific areas of activity with a view to creating targets or goals for performance. Such aspects may include:

* Designing a production range to minimise material wastage.
* Controlling contaminated pollutants in specific production processes.
* Reducing waste in packaging of products for distribution.

As policy lays the foundations for programme development and performance measurement, environmental policy should be developed, where possible, with measurable criteria in mind as this will assist in the development of environmental goals and targets. It is important at this stage, however, that over-detailing should be avoided. Policy should reflect an overall philosophy and commitment with the fine detail reserved for intra-organisational programmes, manuals and documentation.

Policy structure

Environmental management policy should include a clear statement on organisational philosophy, objectives, responsibilities and commitment to the organisation's environmental situation and environmental effects of its business. The core body of policy should embrace the following organisational aspects:

* Scope: describes the organisational view in respect of the achievement of environmental management within those aims and objectives outlined in the *environmental statement* (details follow in this section).
* Corporate responsibility: describes the range and level of responsibility for the potential environmental effects of the organisation's business.
* Legislative accountability: describes adherence to current legislation and regulatory control of business activities in relation to its environmental situation.

- Performance expectations: describes the desired levels of environmental performance with due regard to the above.

These aspects of organisational policy form the basis of a public pronouncement, *the environmental management statement,* of the intentions and principles of action of the organisation in respect of potential environmental effects of its business. Environmental management policy, therefore, is the public face of organisational commitment to the environment, not merely an introspective statement of intent.

(ii) Environmental Statement

An integral part of environmental policy formulation is the completion of an environmental management statement. This is the sole responsibility of strategic management at the highest level. Its accent must embrace the organisation's genuine intentions towards environmental safeguard linked to its aims, objectives, goals and responsibilities. It must form the basis for intra-organisational commitment and engender trust outside the organisation.

As the environmental statement is a public pronouncement, it should be seen as a true representation of organisational principles and intent in a way that the outside world perceives that organisation. It should also be delivered in a way that is commensurate with its audience; it should be clear, precise, simple and understandable and written ostensibly in layman's terms but without being superficial.

Format and presentation
The environmental statement should be a formal statement by the organisation and come from the most senior executive, the company chairman. The statement should be accompanied by the official company letterhead and logo, if applicable, be official in presentation and signed by the chairman. The statement should be a composite part of the policy documentation generated for inclusion in the organisation's environmental management manual. It is also likely that this policy statement will be used in organisational publicity material: for example, yearbooks, annual reports, and promotional documents. It should therefore be written with longevity yet adaptability in mind.

(iii) Aims and Objectives

It was identified in the preceding chapter that an organisation pursuing environmental management should establish and maintain procedures to specify its environmental objectives and further the goals or targets developed from these objectives. The development of environmental aims and objectives is a further duty of strategic management.

Formulation of objectives must be seen to come from the highest level of management within the organisation to establish the following:

- Translation of the organisation's environmental philosophy into clearly focused purpose.
- Development of purpose into defined principles of action.
- Interaction of purpose and principles with the desired management structure and organisation.

In achieving the above it is essential that strategic management ensure that all organisational aims and objectives are consistent with the environmental policy and environmental management statement. Any disparity between objectives and the environmental management statement will undermine the organisation's commitment to environmental issues and therein lose the trust from outside the organisation that is necessary to sustain its commitment and public standing.

(iv) Goals and targets

Further developing the organisational aims and objectives, strategic management are responsible for determining and specifying environmental goals or targets. Goals or targets are developed from environmental objectives by considering the time-scale for implementation of those objectives. Ideally, the organisation should demonstrate its commitment to its environmental policy through continual system improvement and better environmental performance within a set time frame. In practice, improved performance may be feasible in some areas of organisational activity but not others. Similarly, improvements may be desired in some areas more than others. An organisation should therefore target areas where improved performance is beneficial and practicable.

Any organisational goal or target should be quantifiable such that subsequent performance can be easily compared with that desired. In addition, environmental targeting could be linked to personal responsibilities of management and accountability form part of on-going performance appraisal. It may also be beneficial, although not always practical, to link performance to cost benefits and dis-benefits through common systems of cost–benefit analysis as only in this way can achievement be measured to the organisational good.

Goals and targets are inextricably linked with organisational aims and objectives which themselves are intermeshed with organisational policy formulation. The interrelationships of these key aspects should be the prime focus of strategic management in the conceptual development of an environmental management system as they lay all the ground work upon which directive management must develop the system, procedures and working instructions. See Figure 4.6.

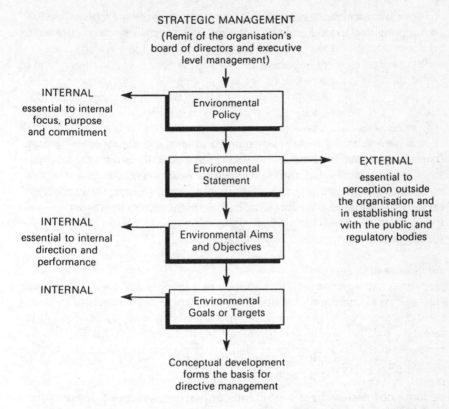

Figure 4.6   Primary functions of strategic management in the development of an environmental management system

Systems development: the functions of directive management

The environmental manager

All aspects reviewed under the heading of directive management should be the responsibility of the environmental manager in the co-ordinating role that is assigned.

(i) Environmental philosophy

Conceptual philosophy and organisational stance will have been determined by strategic management and reflected in the environmental policy. Environmental philosophy at directive management level is concerned with the translation of conceptual aspects into working system aspects as it affects the day-to-day running of the environmental management system.

Environmental management and its attendant systems is concerned with structuring and developing the technical and management competence to achieve the desired levels of environmental performance. It is also concerned with the management of people, embracing the definition and designation of roles, duties and responsibilities of all personnel.

Environmental philosophy should be concerned with managing the sometimes very complex socio-technological interface whilst developing a system of procedures that envelop the total organisational remit of activities. All employees must engender a sense of worth for the environmental management system and hold a considerable commitment to its aims themselves if the system is to develop and be successful in implementation. It is a key role of directive management to provide the necessary philosophy and working environment for the environmental management system to prosper.

(ii) The system

Requirements
Directive management is charged with two primary tasks in the establishment of an environmental management system.

- The preparation of the documented system of procedures and working instructions.
- The effective implementation of the system through managing operational level management.

It is not intended here to prescribe any particular route to developing a specific environmental management system, procedures or working instructions because, first, it is not sensible to prescribe a definite set system to any organisation since all organisations are different and require their own blend of system attributes, and, second, because components for an environmental management system mirror common aspects of all management systems so the basic principles and practices will be well known and accepted.

It is pertinent, however, to mention a number of specific aspects of system development. As documentation and records may be shared between an environmental management system and other organisational systems such as a quality assurance system, the interrelationship between systems should be defined and explained. Where system boundaries cross they should be carefully interfaced to avoid system ambiguity and monitoring and recording mechanisms developed to recognise the requirements of each, both being kept separate to maintain system integrity.

Within environmental systems development, directive management should give timely consideration to identifying skills, equipment and other resources that may be needed to develop the system. Unlike other general management systems, environmental management may necessitate the introduction of environmental monitoring – for example, that needed to assess environmental performance. Such aspects should be built-in to organisational environmental procedures and not introduced retrospectively.

Emphasis

The environmental management system, whatever form it may take, must be designed with an emphasis placed upon the prevention of environmental effects, not merely detection and retrospective management of those affects. This essential requirement demands that any system should focus on procedures and practices which achieve the following:

- Identify and evaluate the potential for environmental effects.
- Determine the environmental effects when they occur.
- Relate the effects to current legislation and regulation.
- Enable firm and realistic performance targets to be set.
- Facilitate planning, control, monitoring and action to be taken.
- Retain sufficient flexibility to meet changing circumstance.

Structure

Developing procedures and working instructions to accommodate the aforementioned requires directive management to carry out the following:

- Define what tasks need to be undertaken.
- Explain why these tasks need to be undertaken.
- Determine when these tasks must be undertaken.
- Control how these tasks are undertaken.
- Identify where the tasks should be undertaken.
- Assign who will undertake these tasks.

These elements can be considered organisationally by developing flow diagrams corresponding to activities within the organisation's system structure. Such flow diagrams can be developed to encompass tasks, procedures to carry out the tasks, and designate responsibilities for the tasks. These system diagrams will form the basis for the documented environmental system manual.

The environmental management system therefore incorporates the following:

- A central flow diagram of organisational structure relating to systems elements.
- Flow sub-diagrams to identify tasks within the system.
- Descriptions to provide detail of the tasks.
- Specification of task procedure to guide the employee through the task in an orderly and uniform manner.
- Job description to identify system areas of, and range of, responsibilities.
- Monitoring and recording mechanisms to be used to provide the system's operational record.

(iii) Environmental programme

Pursuing a defined and well-developed environmental management programme is the key to meeting the requirement of the organisation's environmental policy. As a programme specifies objectives to be obtained, and the
mechanisms for their achievement and can do so in relation to a set time
frame if so desired, the programme should be determined by directive
management for implementation by operational management. Directive
management must therefore ensure that the necessary organisational procedures are in place to facilitate their realisation. It must also provide a timetable
for implementation in the context of the performance expected and by when.
The environmental programme, therefore, will not only be a descriptive
schedule of system expectation but will utilise a typical calendar related
medium; gantt chart; milestone diagram; or similar to record desired progression of activity against programme.

(iv) Organisation and personnel

It is essential for directive management to formulate the system structure and
that there be a clear division between development and implementation. (See
Figures 4.7a and b.) Separation in this way clearly denotes where the responsibilities of directive management and operational management lie. Although
there will be some overlap of directive management through the co-ordinating duties of the environmental manager, there is a clear division in the
environmental programme, directive management creating the programme
and operational management implementing the programme. If this distinction is not made, one is likely to see operational management creating their
own programme and working instructions in the absence of guidance from
directive management, an all too frequent occurrence in consequence of
lacking organisational structure.

In the general formulation of management structure and organisation
illustrated earlier in Figure 4.5, it is pertinent to note that a two-fold approach
may be applicable. Since an organisation will, undoubtedly, undergo continual
change, directive management may develop a central core administrative
structure, the corporate structure and in addition, develop sub-structures
following an activity, perhaps product, process or project based organisation
which can be easily adapted as organisational activity changes and unfolds.
Supplementary to the system task aspects already described, personnel can
be assigned to these structures which then form an integral part of the
environmental management system manual.

(v) Documentation

In the context of environmental systems development, documentation refers
to any informing documents which support procedures or instructions in the

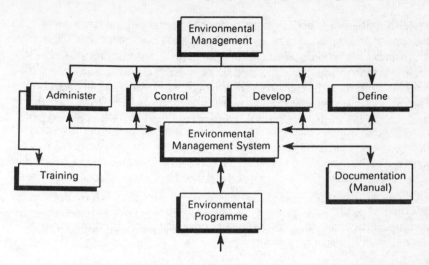

Note: All system aspects shown should be subject to system review and auditing

Figure 4.7a   Structure for organisational development of environmental management system

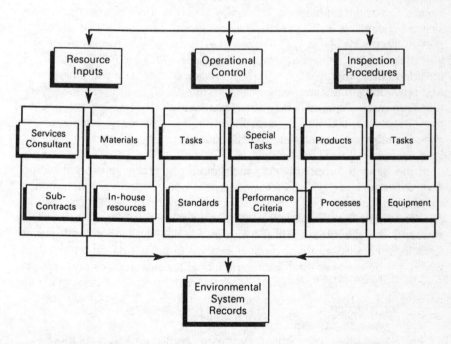

Note: All system aspects shown should be subject to system review and auditing

Figure 4.7b   Structure for organisational implementation of environmental management system

systems manual. It is not uncommon for the content of a systems manual to be supported by guidance notes held in separate document files. These may, for example, provide detailed explanation on key systems procedures where their inclusion in the manual would be beyond the level of detail needed by anyone other than the person to whom it is related. An example might be the use of a job description in the manual. These can be referred to in the manual and their detail filed in separate documents for reference when needed.

(vi) Manual

The environmental management manual, the core system document describing the procedures for implementing the organisation's environmental policy, is the centrepiece of the environmental management system.

Format
Whilst the content of such manuals will vary, determined explicitly by the organisation itself, the constitution of a manual will follow a general format as follows:

- Title leaf.
- Contents list.
- Revision list.
- Distribution list.
- Environmental Statement.
- Summary of manual and instructions for use.
- Environmental Policy description.
- Management structure and organisation.
- Review and audit procedures.
- Reference to supporting documentation.
- Index.

The key areas of this list will be sub-divided and further information to describe and document the environmental management system will be provided as follows:

- Environmental policy
  - Scope.
  - Introduction.
  - Corporate responsibility.
  - Range of responsibilities to standards, legislation and regulations.
  - Management of individuals.
  - Responsibility of individuals.
  - Implementational performance.

- Management structure and organisation
  - The company.
  - The environmental management group structure.
  - Organisation of personnel.
  - Sectional, departmental or divisional responsibilities.
  - Programme.
  - Procedures.
  - Methods of control.
  - Training aspects.
  - System requirements of 'second' organisations (sub-contractors and suppliers).

- Review and audit procedures.
  - Definition of activity.
  - Internal review.
  - Internal audit.
  - External audit.
  - Audit procedures.
  - System update.

Methods of inclusion

The methods of including information in the manual follow those aspects of system development specified. In summary, these are:

- Flow diagrams.
- Flow sub-diagrams.
- Description.
- Specifications.
- Task/job description.
- Pro-forma procedural forms/checklists.

The manual should identify all the primary organisational tasks that need to be performed within the environmental management system. Ideally an individual or group should be identified in association with these tasks and the procedures, working instructions and actions that need to be taken to effect the task should be so described. These descriptions can be aided by flow diagrams and supported by pro-forma procedural forms or checklists for guidance and recording throughout the task. All such aspects are drawn together by the organisation's core or central flow diagram depicting structure throughout the entire environmental management system. An example of a task flow diagram is shown in Figure 4.8.

(vii) Standards

Standards for environmental management systems should be specified within the system manual and cover two levels:

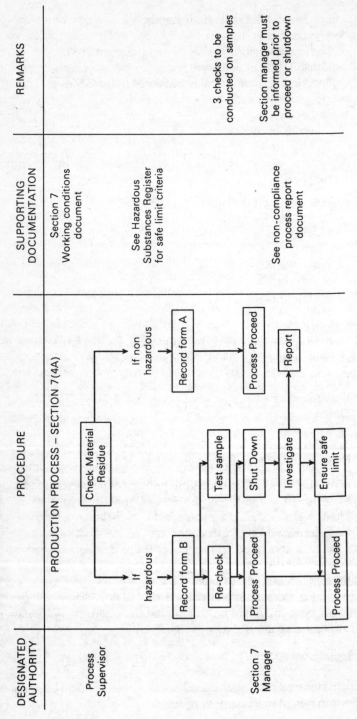

ENVIRONMENTAL MANAGEMENT SYSTEM
SECTION 7: PRODUCTION PROCESS 4A
HAZARDOUS RESIDUE CHECKING PROCEDURE

DESIGNATED AUTHORITY	PROCEDURE	SUPPORTING DOCUMENTATION	REMARKS
Process Supervisor	PRODUCTION PROCESS – SECTION 7(4A) Check Material Residue If non hazardous → Record form A → Process Proceed If hazardous → Record form B → Re-check → Process Proceed Test sample	Section 7 Working conditions document See Hazardous Substances Register for safe limit criteria	
Section 7 Manager	Shut Down → Investigate → Report Ensure safe limit → Process Proceed	See non-compliance process report document	3 checks to be conducted on samples Section manager must be informed prior to proceed or shutdown

Figure 4.8   Example task flow procedure in an environmental management system manual

- System Standards: The system standard for an environmental management system is that given by BS 7750: Specification for Environmental Management Systems.
- Regulatory and Legislative Standards: Any standards of performance specified by regulatory bodies, authorities, institutions and current legislation should be clearly defined and, where appropriate, quantified.

It is the duty of directive level management to ensure that the above are appropriately identified, interpreted correctly and specified accurately for use in the system and incorporated into written statements presented in the system manual (see Figure 4.9).

(viii) Training

It was identified earlier that training is likely to be an important part of environmental management system development. Directive level management is responsible for ensuring that all staff and working personnel are trained in the effective implementation of the system.

Firstly, education of all personnel in the philosophy and conceptual understanding of environmental management is essential to establishing an environmental ethos within the organisation. If system theories fail in practice it is often because of staff and the workforce being unclear as to what the system is attempting to achieve and how their involvement is vital to its existence.

Initial staff training should be focused upon providing the appropriate and correct resources at the right time to ensure that the workforce can best operate the system. Specialised personnel training should follow to ensure that procedures and working practice are undertaken efficiently and effectively.

Training is, however, an on-going organisational commitment, and educational packages in the form of continuing professional development, on-the-job instruction and brainstorming activities may be needed to maintain management and personnel awareness of system operations, review and update.

4.4 Implementation

Implementation stage

The implementation stage of environmental management systems should satisfy the requirements of the following systems elements:

- Operational control.
- Environmental management records.
- Environmental management audits.
- Environmental management reviews.

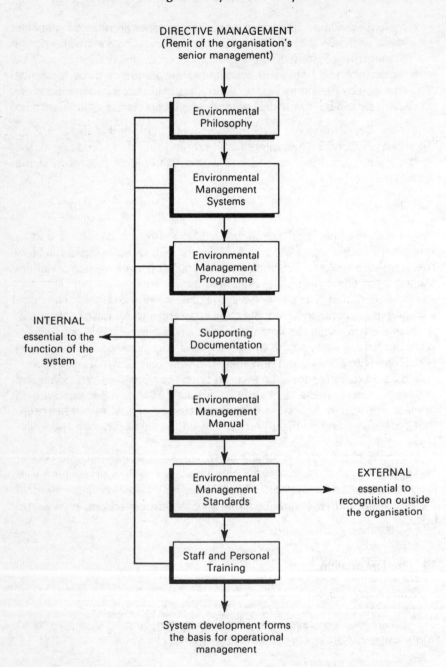

Figure 4.9   Primary function of directive management in the development of an environmental management system

There will also be some overlap with systems elements in the development stage (see section 4.3).

Fulfilling the above requirements is essentially the task of operational management, the first-line supervisors who operate and monitor the system on a day-to-day basis. It was identified in section 4.3 that their remit addresses four primary tasks, which meet not only the four system elements specified above but, when combined with the preceding seven specified system elements of the development stage, form a total environmental management system. (See Figure 4.10.)

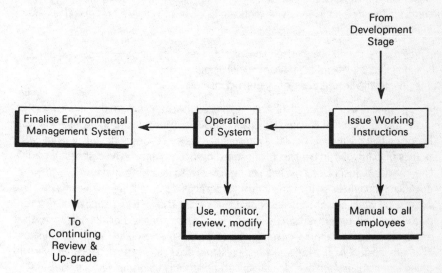

Figure 4.10   The implementation stage of environmental management systems development and implementation

The functions that Operational management should address are:

- Operation of the system.
- Monitoring.
- Record keeping.
- Provision of feedback.

System implementation: the functions of operational management

(i) Operation of the system

Circulation of the systems manual

It is essential to the general operation of the environmental management system that, ideally all personnel, but certainly those persons holding responsibility for aspects of the system have a copy of the environmental management system manual.

Control

In developing the environmental management system, the organisation will have identified functions, activities and the processes which have a potential effect upon the environment. The organisation will also have considered the undertaking of these with minimum risk through the detailed analysis of procedures. It is these procedures which form the core of the systems manual. Described in terms of working information these achieve the following:

- Provide guidance to the individual.
- Facilitate control by system supervisors.
- Assure management of system continuity and standards.

Operation and control of the system is conducted to the documented work instructions of the organisation's environmental management manual. Responsibilities for particular system activities are described, together with points of control and methods of recording performance. As discussed earlier, the manual describes the set procedures and working instructions and, in addition, provides annotated flow diagrams to facilitate ease of use. The accent of such system implementation is that the whole process or discrete parts of it can be continuously monitored and recorded and, moreover, that any activity or problems can be traced back to source through the system. The environmental management system, like all system theories, should provide a comprehensive documented approach to organisational activity.

(ii) Monitoring

A key function of operational management, in association with directive management, is the monitoring of the system. Monitoring is essential to the maintenance of the system and vital to the early identification and diagnosis of those difficulties and problems which will undoubtedly occur in the operation of the environmental management system.

The primary tasks of monitoring are to:

- Identify problems when they occur.
- Determine their cause.
- Formulate a plan of action.
- Initiate preventive action.
- Apply control measures.
- Realise any change to procedures resulting from corrective actions.

The essential attributes of effective monitoring procedures are:

- Continuity.
- Uniformity.
- Recordability.

These aspects form the basis of verification, non-compliance and corrective action responses, pre-requisite to BS 7750 under operational control.

(iii) Record keeping

Records are the tangible evidence of environmental management system operation. It is often assumed that all system theories demand bureaucratic methods supported by overwhelming amounts of paperwork. To some extent this is true, but in practice care should be taken to ensure that record keeping is limited to an extent commensurate with the application and need for traceability. All records, however, should be kept in order, indexed and filed, irrespective of the recording medium, and designed primarily to relate to and demonstrate compliance with the organisation's environmental policy.

Operational management should ensure that, where records are compiled under shared management systems, this is duly noted and indexed for retrieval purposes. An important factor of operational management is to keep directive management updated on system operations to monitor the organisation's register of environmental effects. This can only be achieved through accurate recording of activities monitored. As discussed in the previous chapter, specification for record keeping demands that all environmental records should be legible, and identifiable to activity, product or service involved. They must be stored such that they are easily retrieved and protected against damage, deterioration and loss.

(iv) Provision of feedback

The provision of feedback from environmental management systems from operational management to higher management level is achieved ostensibly through a system of audit procedures.

Audits

The environmental management manual should specify the method and frequency of auditing. Audits should cover both administrative management and organisational business, activities, the product or service outputs. Auditing mechanisms should co-ordinate both internal auditing by the organisation itself and external auditing.

There is frequent ambiguity as to what constitutes internal and external auditing and how audits differ from review.

Review:

Is an examination by the organisation's environmental manager and team, to assess the effectiveness of the environmental management system and to implement change if activity is not to the required procedures, working instructions or standards.

Audit:

Is an independent examination of the environmental management system to provide assurance to strategic management (and external parties) that the environmental management system is effective in implementation and complies with policy, procedures, instructions and standards.

Internal audit is therefore essentially review or self-assessment whilst external audit is that undertaken by an external party, be it a consultant appointed by the organisation or regulatory body.

Internal audit (review) carried out by the organisation may seek to examine the whole system or parts of the system. They may, therefore, be conducted in any of the following:

- The whole environmental management system.
- Organisational divisions.
- Organisational departments.
- Organisational sections.
- Specific activities.
- Particular products or services.
- Activities of 'second' organisations (sub-contractors/suppliers).

In all cases, auditing procedures should be co-ordinated by the environmental manager. This is emphasised further where external audits are to be conducted as the environmental manager forms the vital integrating link between the organisation and the audit team.

The purpose of audits are to determine that the policy, aims and objectives are being met and being effectively implemented by all divisions, departments and sections within the structure of the organisation.

The environmental manager should arrange all audits. This can be done verbally and confirmed in writing, and should be followed up by a check list (agenda) of the principal aspects within the organisation which are to be audited. In practice the auditors, if external, will request documentation from the environmental management system to be made available before the audit visit and a list of queries prepared. Audits follow a visit to the organisation during which the formal examination of the system, manual and documentation will be made. The findings of the auditors should be made at the end of the visit, reinforced by a written report describing any non-conformance or problems which the organisation must address within the time frame for rectification (see Figure 4.11).

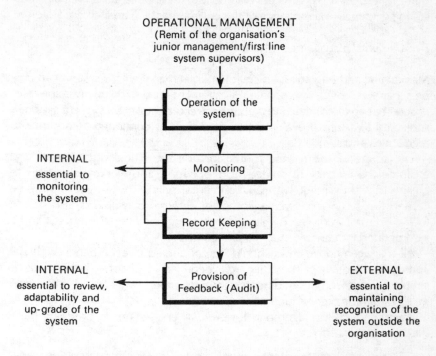

Figure 4.11   Primary functions of operational management in the development and implementation of an environmental management system

Following audit, it is the responsibility of the environmental manager to ensure that any non-conformances are addressed, that the system is upgraded to accommodate revised procedures and that operational management is provided with the necessary resources and training to effect revised working practices.

Further detailed information on auditing and managing audit procedures can be obtained from BS 7229 (Parts 1, 2, and 3).[2]

Drawing the system together

Within this chapter, Figures 4.1, 4.2, 4.3 and 4.10 have illustrated the composite parts of environmental management system development, namely Initiation, Investigation, Development and Implementation. Description of each aspect has presented a schematic outline to create an environmental management system. Figure 4.12 presents an schematic overview of the whole process of systems development and implementation. It can be seen from this diagram that one aspect of systems development and implementation remains out-standing, namely maintenance of the environmental management system.

Environmental management reviews

Maintaining and upgrading an environmental management system can only be achieved through appropriate management review. The organisation must ensure that at appropriate intervals the environmental management system is subjected to a formal evaluation to determine its continued compliance to regulations and standards.

The scope of the review should include the whole organisation and evaluate the efficacy of objectives, procedures and working practices to ensure that they meet with environmental policy. These reviews may be carried out by internal management or external consultants and should follow external audit such that recommendations from the audit can be incorporated into revised systems procedures.

All management reviews should be conducted in accordance with the appropriate section of the standards, identified in Chapter 3, and findings should be recorded in documented form for action by all levels of manage-ment within the organisation.

Environmental Management Reviews will ensure, on an on-going basis, that:

- The environmental management system and its documentation ade-quately accommodates the needs of the organisation.
- The system procedures are practical, understood and followed by both directive and operational management.
- The training provisions at operational levels are satisfactory.
- The necessary resources are being committed to system operation and maintenance.
- The system continues to meet prevailing environmental circumstances.
- The system meets current regulatory requirements.
- The system provides the best way of meeting the challenge of its environmental and market situation.

4.5   Extending existing management systems

BS 7750: Specification for Environmental Management Systems

The specification applicable to the development and implementation of environmental management systems, BS 7750, is designed to enable any

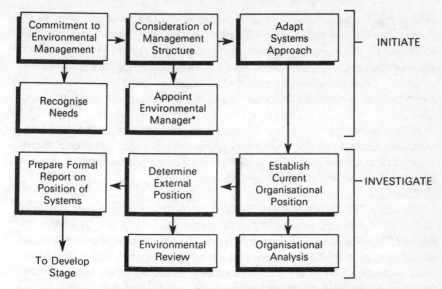

* BS 7750 specifies appointment of 'Environmental Management Representative'

Figure 4.12a   Systems approach to environmental management

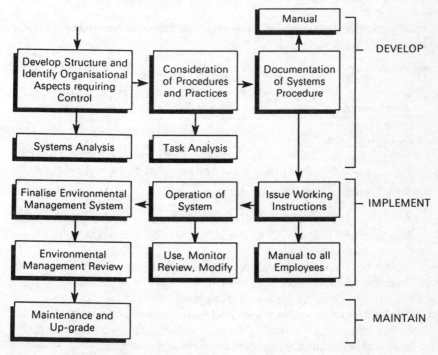

Figure 4.12b   Systems approach to environmental management

organisation to establish a management system as the basis for ensuring safe environmental performance and for participation in environmental auditing schemes. BS 7750 presents common management system principles which are, in essence, shared with BS 5750, the UK's national standard specification for quality systems.[3] An organisation may decide to use an existing management system, developed to BS 5750, as a basis for environmental management.

Adaptation of BS 5750 may require reference to other guidance documentation, for example sector application guidance and regulatory requirements appertaining to the particular business activities, such as production processes. Attention is drawn to this need.

Links to BS 5750: Quality Systems

Figure 4.13 indicates the close linkage between system application sub-clauses of BS 5750 and BS 7750. Where linkage is apparent an organisation can usefully adopt BS 5750 specification, subject to the additional requirements for environmental management systems being adopted also. In all cases of shared systems elements or activities, the interrelationship should be explained and referenced with the respective systems manuals and documentation.

Similarities in standards and additional requirements of an environmental management system

4.1   *Environmental Management System*
Similarities between Standards – system, procedures and instructions comparable, both reliant upon organisation's commitment to system approach.

4.2   *Environmental Policy*
Similarities between Standards – policies comparable. Additional requirements: environmental policy should be supported by environmental objectives, quantified where possible.

4.3   *Organisation and Personnel*
Similarities between Standards – requirements comparable, both recognise specialist management representative to be appointed.

4.4   *Environmental Effects*
Similarities between Standards – no direct similarity, some loose indirect links (see BS 5750/7750).

4.5   *Environmental Objectives and Targets*
Similarities between Standards – purpose broadly similar in that they define levels of organisational performance. Additional requirements: environmental objectives and targets are more wide-ranging.

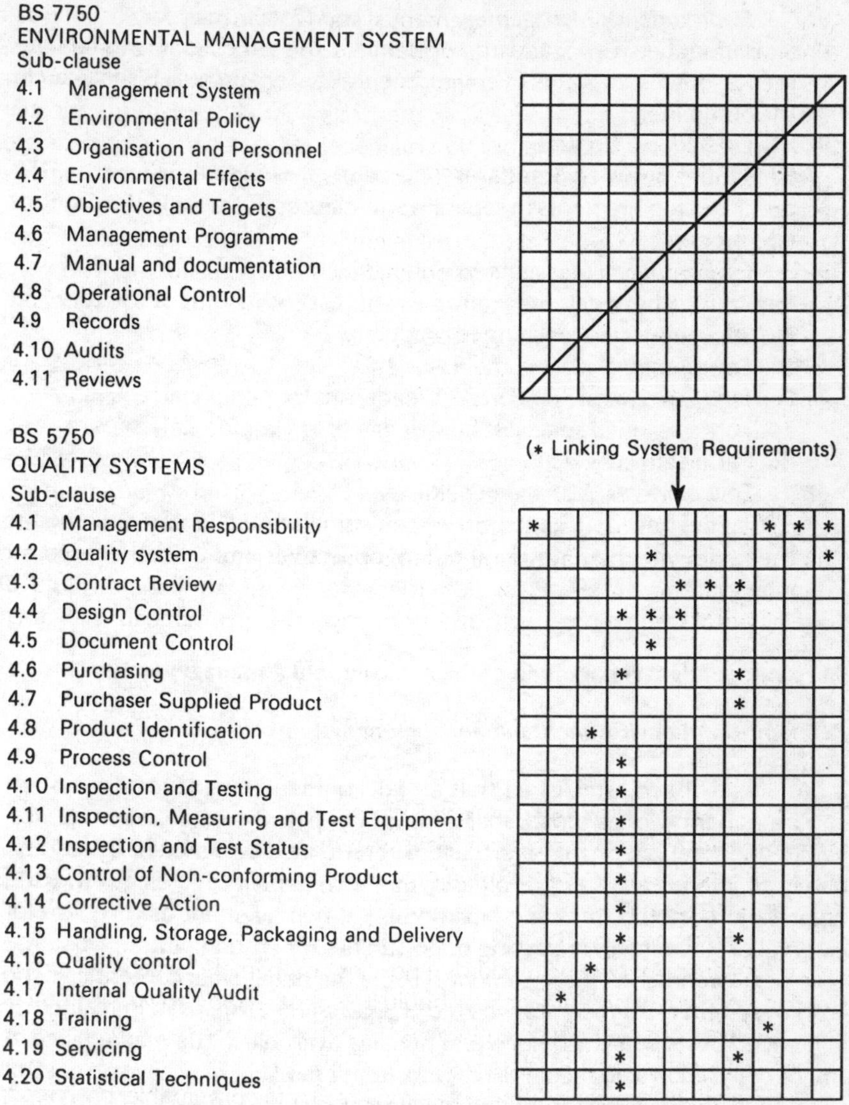

BS 7750
ENVIRONMENTAL MANAGEMENT SYSTEM
Sub-clause

4.1 Management System
4.2 Environmental Policy
4.3 Organisation and Personnel
4.4 Environmental Effects
4.5 Objectives and Targets
4.6 Management Programme
4.7 Manual and documentation
4.8 Operational Control
4.9 Records
4.10 Audits
4.11 Reviews

BS 5750
QUALITY SYSTEMS
Sub-clause

(∗ Linking System Requirements)

4.1 Management Responsibility
4.2 Quality system
4.3 Contract Review
4.4 Design Control
4.5 Document Control
4.6 Purchasing
4.7 Purchaser Supplied Product
4.8 Product Identification
4.9 Process Control
4.10 Inspection and Testing
4.11 Inspection, Measuring and Test Equipment
4.12 Inspection and Test Status
4.13 Control of Non-conforming Product
4.14 Corrective Action
4.15 Handling, Storage, Packaging and Delivery
4.16 Quality control
4.17 Internal Quality Audit
4.18 Training
4.19 Servicing
4.20 Statistical Techniques

Figure 4.13   Links between specification requirements of BS 7750 and BS 5750

4.6   Environmental Management Programme

Similarities between Standards – both concerned with meeting contractual requirements. Additional requirements: environmental management programme is more wide ranging to meet broader objectives.

4.7   Environmental Management Manual and Documentation
Similarities between Standards – essentially the same. Additional requirements: outline contents of environmental system manual is specified in
the Standard.

4.8   Operational Control
Similarities between Standards – no corresponding sub-clause BS 5750
describes requirements in separate sub-clauses as stages in the production process.

4.9   Environmental Management Records
Similarities between Standards – both essentially the same BS 5750
includes sub-clauses relating to products.

4.10   Environmental Management Audits
Similarities between Standards – broadly similar. Additional requirements:
auditors may need specialist knowledge of environmental issues to conduct audit effectively.

4.11   Environmental Management Reviews
Similarities between Standards – broadly similar. Additional requirements:
the review of environmental policy, objectives and targets should be
inherent.

4.6   Independent recognition of the environmental management system

Recognition of environmental management systems

It has already been established that an environmental management system
can be as narrow or as broad, shallow or as deep as the organisation desires.
Whilst one organisation may feel that environmental management is predomi-
nately an internal aspect of its organisation with benefits accruing within the
organisation, another may see environmental management as a vehicle for
external exploitation in marketing opportunities for ensuring future work. The
type of environmental management system, the detail of its content and the
level of system recognition to which the organisation aspires is, in real terms,
influenced by its perceived need and benefits available in the marketplace. A
small organisation who secures all its work from one client may have no need at
all to develop an environmental management system if the client is satisfied
with the arrangement, whereas a larger company wishing to secure work from
major clients may need environmental management to satisfy the pre-qualification demands set by that client in the commercial marketplace. The main
point is that system recognition should be commensurate with need.

Level of assessment

There are, essentially, three levels of system recognition to which an environmental management system, like other systems, can be related:

(i)   First Party:
       where an organisation sees its implemented system as an internal one, but when tendering for work it can notify a potential client that it has a recognised environmental management system.

(ii)   Second Party:
       where an organisation may develop its system in collaboration with its client, or has an internal system open to client scrutiny when tendering for work with that client.

(iii) Third Party:
       where an organisation's system is assessed by an external authoritative (certification) body and is recognised as having a system that meets authoritative specification standards (BS 7750).

An organisation must decide for itself the level of recognition it seeks for its system. Those that wish to meet the criteria of third-party recognition will be involved with the following aspects:

Certification

Certification is:

'The act of licensing by a document formally attesting the fulfilment of conditions.' (BS 4478)

In simple terms, an organisation must develop and implement a documented system that meets those criteria set by an independent body.
   The independent or external bodies that ensure compliance of the system are 'certification bodies'. These are:

'An impartial body, governmental or non-governmental possessing the necessary competence and reliability to operate a certification scheme and in which the interest of the parties concerned with the functioning system are represented.' (DTI)

These bodies therefore vet the system presented by an organisation.

Accreditation

Certification bodies are themselves approved and controlled by Government (Accreditation). Accreditation is:

'The formal recognition by a national government against published criteria, of the technical competence and impartiality of a certification body or testing laboratory.' (NACCB)

In practice governmental control is delegated to the National Accreditation Council for Certification Bodies (NACCB), a representative office of the Department of Trade and Industry (DTI). Essentially this body provides a uniform system of approval for all certification (approval) schemes, i.e. those schemes to which an organisation presents its system for approval is itself approved by government assuming national recognition of the scheme and the systems vetted by it.

Environmental management certification and accreditation

The recognition of environmental management systems through certification is currently at an evolutionary stage and matters are made all the more fraught since harmonisation of practice across the European Community (EC) is yet to be fully realised.

In the UK, third-party assessment of environmental management systems looks set to follow the trend of quality systems certification to BS 5750 standards through accredited certification bodies. As it has been seen, BS 7750 is consistent with the approach of BS 5750 and also satisfies many of the criteria of certification schemes for environmental auditing (eco-management and auditing) within the EC.

As third-party assessment and recognition of environmental management systems develops within the UK it is more than likely that the National Accreditation Council for Certification Bodies (NACCB) and Association of Certification Bodies (ACB) will become the overseeing accreditation bodies while the British Standards Institution and other private organisations will register as certification bodies. This would further the well established and accepted pattern seen in quality system certification.

Given this situation, two aspects of environmental management practice should be the prime objective of an organisation:

(i) The development and implementation of a system to BS 7750.
(ii) The pursuit of independent recognition (certification) for that system.

Applying for certification

It is not the intention here to digress into a discourse of how an organisation applies for certification of its environmental management system. The approach will follow closely that already well known and accepted in quality system certification, and if the reader is not familiar with this, a number of references in Sources of Further Information can provide guidance in this respect. In addition, the reader is directed to authoritative guidance within published documents from BSI.

Value of environmental management certification

With an effective environmental management system an organisation should accrue the benefit of improved environmental operation and efficiency. Environmental effects should be reduced and the standing of the organisation in the longer term should be enhanced. Internal, first or second party, environmental management systems will undoubtedly lead to some advantages, but greater benefits can be achieved where the organisation pursues third-party recognition of its environmental management system.

Benefits will accrue from:

- A system that meets the recognised requirements of an authoritative body at national level (certification body) and one that meets a well-accepted standard (BS 7750) will be recognised locally, nationally and internationally.
- The long-term commitment to environmental issues recognised by commercial clients, financiers, insurers, regulatory bodies and the public.
- Listing in governmental registers of environmentally sound organisations both nationally and internationally.
- Registration in a list of organisations made publically available by the certification bodies.
- The use of the certification scheme's recognised logo recognising environmental management achievement.

Given the potential benefits to an organisation that implements an environmental management system, as identified in Chapter 1, an organisation simply cannot ignore the weight of evidence leading them towards third-party external recognition of their system. However, there are a number of detrimental aspects that can lead to considerable concern, even scepticism, when formulating a potential environmental management system. These follow subsequently.

European standards and certification for environmental management

Since the early 1990s the accent across Europe has been to unify standards in all fields of business and commerce and harmonise certification to allow products and services access to commercial markets through unified practices. The primary mechanisms for these are EC Directives which, in simple terms, become national legislation in member countries. The CE Mark, attributed to many products, confirms that a product conforms to the applicable EC Directives. In this way, such products can become subject to any requirement stipulated by the EC Directive including specifications for environmental aspects.

European standards (EN) represents the national standard across member countries and are the vehicle for invoking EC Directives. Each member country has established certification bodies similar to those recognised in the UK, although in Europe these are known as *Notified Bodies*.

European standards (EN) evolve from standards developed by the European Committee for Standardisation (CEN). Their standards become EN standards and apply across member countries to ensure uniformity.

It is, of course, easier to invoke such standards and directives on products since they are manufactured under controlled conditions to well-specified and well-marshalled standards. Management aspects such as environmental systems, however, are more difficult to regulate since allegiance to environmental management certification schemes is voluntary and is market driven rather than legislatively driven.

There is little doubt however that, in the same way that BS 5750: quality systems has become widespread in use in the UK and become harmonised within the EC to accompany EN 29000 and the International Standards Organisation ISO 9000 Series, environmental management is set to proliferate on an international scale.

European Community (EC), eco-management and auditing scheme

EC member countries participate in eco-management and eco-auditing schemes under current EC directives. These require that an organisation:

- Develops and implements an internal environmental management system.
- That the organisation evaluates the performance of that system.
- That they keep the public advised of their environmental performance and environmental effects that occur.
- That they issue an environmental statement which is externally audited.

These demands essentially follow those outlined in a BS 7750 system where, of course, auditing and wider recognition of environmental management systems are key features.

Implications of environmental management system certification

Organisations will encounter two main concerns when formulating an environmental management system:

(i) The *time* involved to develop and implement the system.
(ii) The *costs*, both direct and indirect.

Time

The time to develop, implement, evaluate and refine an environmental management system in order to be able to apply for external recognition (certification), will vary from organisation to organisation depending upon its size, business activities, operating procedures and its workload. Whilst one cannot be precise, a small organisation is likely to find that the evolutionary period for environmental management system development and implementation will be at least twelve months and probably between one to two years. The problem is not so much that systems need to be developed, as they probably already exist; the difficulty lies in documentating those procedures, refining them and finalising optimum working instructions. In addition, it is not enough to develop and implement the system; it must run and be monitored over a period of time to ensure that it operates effectively.

A likely timetable will see the first six months involved in developing new or amending existing procedures, the next six months will be involved in documenting those procedures, a further six months in trial running, monitoring and refinement and this is all before the organisation embarks upon seeking external recognition. The certification process itself could take many months to complete.

Cost

Unfortunately, the potential benefits that may be accrued by the organisation through the establishment of an environmental management system cannot be secured without cost and this can be high. There are the fixed costs resulting from the formulation of the system and certification processes should an organisation pursue third-party recognition and then the variable costs of running the system within a changing environment. Significant costs are incurred in:

- Developing the environmental management system procedures.
- Producing the documentation and environmental management manual.
- Implementation and monitoring of the system.
- Maintaining an internal audit system.
- Undertaking external audits, where appropriate.
- Independent third-party assessment and certification, if pursued.

These major expenditures are one-off and on-going costs. It is difficult to be precise as to what constitutes fixed or variable costs since experience with quality systems has shown that costs are changeable, difficult to budget for and, in reality, an organisation rarely determines the true cost of development and implementation since many costs are hidden or lost intra-organisationally. Based on '1994 prices' an organisation could expect to spend anything between £600 and £3000 per employee in setting up and implementing an environmental management system with annual running costs generating additional expenditure. These figures take into account the fact that many organisations will procure the services of consultants to advise on system development.

Where an organisation can rely on in-house development, costs will be lower and, of course, reductions would be expected in a larger organisation where economies of scale are likely to exert a beneficial effect. A substantial reduction should be expected where the environmental management system is extended from an existing management system as the main cost will have already been expended. In most eventualities, cost remains a prohibitive factor to all systems applications.

Cost–benefit analysis

Since most all organisations treat the matter of cost and time expenditure on systems development with overwhelming sensitivity, it is no surprise to learn that little cost–benefit analytical information is available. It is interesting to note that some organisations formulating environmental management systems are following the trend seen in quality systems where the organisation is not regarding environmental management in cost–benefit terms specifically but is defining environmental management as an organisational necessity and appreciating the benefits that are accrued as a bonus to organisational effectiveness and efficiency.

4.7   Developmental issues: concerns and problems associated with environmental management systems development

Research study

The developmental issues, or concerns and problems associated with environmental management systems development, presented in this section, have been determined from the following:

- *Research Study*: conducted in the course of compiling this book.
- *Sources*: a number of UK national and multinational based companies who are currently implementing, or have begun to develop, environmental management systems.
- *Biography*: material is derived from two broad approaches by organisations:
  (a) Those developing an environmental management system.
  (b) Those extending an existing management system.
- *Other information*: has been obtained from recent empirical sources and organisations working in the field of environmental management.

Focus

The developmental issues raised can be broadly categorised into three groups:

(i)   Those exclusive to the development and implementation of environmental management systems.
(ii) Those already clearly identified and well recognised in the course of
developing and implementing existing management systems experience, with BS 5750: Quality Systems being the prominent source.
(iii) Those characteristics to any system theory development and
implementation.

Classification

To assist clarity of focus and ease of discussion, the concerns and problems
encountered, or likely to be encountered, in environmental management
systems development are diagnosed in terms of management level within
an organisation. This maintains continuity with the preceding material in
this chapter. These management levels are: (i) *Strategic*, (ii) *Directive* and (iii)
Operational, although it is acknowledged that it may not always be practicable nor appropriate to categorise in this way. There will always be concerns
and problems that do not fall conveniently into particular pigeon-holes of
management responsibility.

Manifestation

Developmental issues fall into one of two broad types:

(i)   Those that are known to exist from actual experience in systems development.
(ii) Those that are anticipated to occur in environmental management
systems development.

Limitations

The development issues which follow do not represent an exhaustive list, nor
are they prioritised in importance or other aspect. They serve to provide some
level of insight into concerns that have been expressed and problems which
have occurred, or are likely to be encountered, in the course of environmental
management systems development and implementation.

A. Strategic

At the strategic management level there is considerable evidence to suggest
that an organisation is likely to encounter the following conceptual concerns
and problems:

- *Management scepticism:*
  The absence of 'top-down' management is perhaps the most unstabling and debilitating element in environmental systems development. It is certainly the most fundamental organisational weakness. 'Management' must come from the top and be seen to come from the top. The biggest commitment must be from executive management who must develop clear and unambiguous policy and objectives, be approachable, listen to the problems which are inevitable and actively lead staff to overcome difficulties throughout the organisation. The organisation must perceive the need for and *want* environmental management, and not merely react with reluctance or respond to a trend. The holistic conceptualisation of environmental management is formed from the organisation's basic philosophy and this itself is created by the highest level of management.

- *Diversity of organisational activity:*
  Accommodating the many diverse activities within an organisation can be problematic, in particular within the larger organisation which can be both broad and deep. In concept, an environmental management system seeks to encompass the whole organisation, yet in practice it is often more feasible and manageable to develop systems which, in the short term, can be readily applied to discrete parts of the organisation and in the longer term be easily extended to other parts of the organisation. Difficulties are seen to arise where these parts, or sub-systems, fail to maintain uniformity or continuity across the wider environmental management system. Strategic management should consider this within the programme of short, medium and longer-term environmental system development.

- *Organisational commitment:*
  An environmental management system will, undoubtedly, come under pressure to perform well, if not perfectly, and to establish procedures quickly, if not immediately. The reality is, of course, that it takes time and money to develop a *workable* system. Although the developmental learning curve should be as short as practicable, the environmental management system should not be implemented until there is organisational conviction and commitment to its form and nature. It is all too easy to encourage ridicule from both management and the workforce if senior management implement a system which has not been fully thought through at strategic level or has not been fully developed because it has been rushed or denied adequate resources.

- *Financial implications:*
  The financial burden upon an organisation when developing any management system is considerable. Experience with quality assurance systems has demonstrated that while the cost profile declines in the

longer term, start-up costs can appear excessive. For many organisations a system cost, equated in terms of per employee, would be between £1000 to £3000 (indexed in 1994). In addition, there will be an on-going expense of maintaining the system and further cost if an organisation seeks to register its system with an appropriate certification body. Although there will be some reduction through economies of scale (the more employees the organisation has, the more economic the system will be), systems in general are, prima facie, cost prohibitive. With regard to environmental management systems there is, at the time of writing this book, no tangible cost–benefit analysis data available to establish the true cost and worth of environmental management systems to an organisation. Experience has shown that systems management approaches, in the main, do make the organisation more efficient and therefore cost-effective. An environmental management system should be no less beneficial. One however may choose not to equate benefit directly with cost. Many organisations perceive the need to respond to market forces or changes in legislation such that they develop an environmental management system irrespective of the cost implications. As has been the case with quality management systems, environmental management systems might be looked upon more appropriately in terms of being simply good for business, securing the organisation's position in the marketplace and focusing business policy upon the maximisation of turnover and long-term profit base.

- *Organisational change:*
One of the more daunting practical issues for strategic management to address is that of eliciting support for organisational change. The earliest experiences with quality management showed that resistance to concepts and applications clearly hindered its early development and widespread adoption as an accepted management tool. The organisational change necessitated by environmental management systems is more demanding than even that which was required in the early development of quality systems. Experience in systems development has shown that organisational change is primarily hindered by poor communications, resulting in both management and employees not understanding how and why the system is operating. Senior management must develop an organisational ethos which encapsulates understanding, attention and commitment of the workforce. It is essential to introduce an environmental management system with pertinence and with empathy for those who must operate it and not merely invoke a system that will be met with fear and resistance.

- *Superficial environmental review:*
An environmental management system is unlikely to be successful where the organisation's preparatory environmental review has been

superficial or inadequate. Certainly, with quality management systems, organisations encountered overwhelming difficulty where senior management were unsure of where their organisation stood in the marketplace or in which direction they felt their organisation should go in meeting the demands for quality assurance. Similarly, environmental management demands that an organisation accurately sets its benchmark, asks itself specific questions and addresses certain fundamental issues prior to embarking upon environmental management systems development. Environmental review may be too superficial or inadequate for its intended purposes due to management indecision, lack of knowledge or experience or a real lack of understanding of the organisation or environmental management system requirements. Strategic management must be clear on the range of issues discussed in section 4.2 before seeking to develop an environmental management system.

- *Extension of existing management systems:*
In the same way that environmental management systems can be developed by extending existing organisational management systems, in the early development of quality management systems they too were often developed by adapting existing management systems. Experience in quality management has shown that extending or adapting existing systems leads to a tendency for the organisation to operate the systems in parallel rather than being fully integrated. Whilst environmental management may be developed along similar lines to other organisational systems, its focus must take account of the individual needs of the organisation and its environment. Each system is therefore specific to the organisation. Problems are likely to result where this is not appreciated or where this is given insufficient attention. An organisation may take one of three routes to system development: (i) adopt a generic system blindly; (ii) borrow a system inappropriately; (iii) develop a system pertinent to its organisation and activities. In reality, only the third option will lead to successful development and implementation of an environmental management system.

- *Public scrutiny:*
A major issue that many organisations need to come to terms with is the public aspect of environmental management systems. Environmental management is the public face of the organisation's care for, action toward and commitment to the environment, and an organisation can come under the closest scrutiny by third parties; regulatory bodies; legislative councils; protection agencies; and the public. Occasionally the organisation is likely to find itself defending its actions openly, particularly in an emergency situation, say a pollution violation. Public relations and media handling is an aspect which all but the best practised organisations do with ease and competence. An organisation's most

senior management must appreciate that their environmental policy and environmental statement is the yardstick by which they will be judged, not just intra and inter organisationally, but in the outside world.

B. Directive

There is a weight of evidence to suggest that an organisation is likely to encounter the following developmental concerns and problems at the directive management level:

* *Education and training:*
  Research has shown unequivocally that where education and training has been absent or inadequate during environmental management systems development, implementation has not been successful. Education and training for environmental management systems development and implementation is simply prerequisite at all organisational levels and for management staff and the workforce. Some degree of education in systems theory and application is needed even at the highest management levels. Research has indicated that often strategic management will know where they wish the organisation to go but have insufficient knowledge in how to steer that chosen course. Strategic management should have more than a mere conceptual understanding of the environmental management system, although it is accepted that their role and responsibilities are essentially at a conceptual level. Strategic and directive management must be trained in the dynamics of their system, be approachable to deal with the problems confronting operational management and be available to guide and support from a sound knowledge base. This requires that executive and directive management are trained, to some degree, not necessarily in the hands-on use of the system, but in the functioning of the system and implications that arise from its use.

  Directive management should assume responsibility for systems education and training at all levels, strategic, directive and operational. Training will be a function of the environmental manager or directive management in personnel, if the system is sufficiently large to maintain a personnel department. This should follow a structured and evolving pattern of education needs.

  There are indications from some system applications already that where there has been little or no training in the philosophy of the undertaking, then this has undermined the early stages of development with severe knock-on effects in implementation. Systems training must commence with basic education at an indoctrine level to introduce and develop the philosophical and conceptual issues of the environmental management system. This lays the foundation for organisational support upon which system education and training can be positively delivered.

Perhaps the single most important issue highlighted is that directive management must overcome resistance and scepticism often born from fear, that a systems approach seeks to undermine, even displace, the individual when, in fact, the system can aid and support the individual. It has been clearly identified that initial systems training is best concentrated on understanding resource requirements and making a new system compatible with existing functions such that the system is not invoked but that it almost introduces and consolidates itself into the general working programme.

Early environmental management systems, like early quality systems, have, to some extent, followed a 'Learn as you go' approach and while this is somewhat inevitable to a degree, training should follow a structured organisational approach. It was identified that where a new environmental management system was being developed, training almost had to develop alongside the system. This is not, in itself, a bad thing given that all systems suffer from operational change such as staff turnover or amended working practices, and thus training is seen as an on-going activity that through a pattern of continuing professional development (CPD) should maintain relevance and currency.

- *Management responsibility:*
  In the development of an environmental management system the bulk of responsibility lies with the environmental manager, a directive-level position. Like many 'middle' management posts the directive-level manager may be forced, by organisational circumstances, to adopt a dual role where competing demands lead to compromised effectiveness of role and function. In system applications generally and seen many times in quality systems development, directive management frequently has too wide an authority with poorly defined role, duties and responsibilities. In such circumstances system efficacy cannot be maintained to any great degree. It is paramount at directive level generally and in the context of an environmental management system, that the environmental manager has a clarity of role and organisational position.

- *Interpreting standards in the context of the organisation:*
  BS 7750 is generic in as much as its potential application can be as narrow or as broad as an organisation requires and be applied across a wide range of business activities in many sectors. As such, it requires careful interpretation and pertinent application if it to be used effectively. Problems occur where an organisation attempts to use its concepts *per se*. Rather, the specification for environmental management systems should be used in the context of the organisation as a management tool aimed at providing a systematic approach towards better environmental management.

Many problems followed the introduction of BS 5750 Quality Systems, as organisations sought to implement the standard without taking into account the individual characteristics and needs of their business nor the market sectors in which they operate. The environmental management system must blend the many characteristics of the organisation with the world surrounding that organisation. This is a function of directive management who translate corporate policy and objectives into procedures and working practices through environmental management system development and documentation.

- *Start-up resources:*
Although it is impossible to provide an indication in quantitative terms, it is well accepted that the start-up costs of an environmental management system will be high. This is particularly true where the organisation is essentially developing a new system with no similar organisational systems to draw upon. Where an existing system is being modified to suit the requirements of an environmental management system, the early development costs have already been incurred and only modest start-up costs will be incurred. The bulk of these costs are likely to be consumed by additional staffing and the training of both new and existing staff to systems operations.

- *Bureaucratic management:*
System theories of any kind raise fears among management of bureaucracy, over-management, excessive paperwork and systematisation. Although some of these aspects may indeed appear within proportion, fear is generally unsubstantiated in systems implementation. The organisation should be ready to handle the early scepticism and resentment that will undoubtedly occur initially but recognise that this is merely an inevitable manifestation of organisational change that will peter out as procedures become second nature to both management and personnel.

- *Communication with operational management:*
Research in environmental management systems and, moreover, in quality systems has shown that system development is weak where the system is unclear to directive management, the very people who must instil understanding and support in operational-level management. Operational management need early guidance. This comes from directive management being clear on systems requirements but, moreover, depends upon their ability to communicate and inform. Because system development is usually a learning process for all management levels, directive management must display a willingness to empathise with operational management to develop systems aspects that have the best chance of being successful in implementation.

C. Operational

There is considerable evidence to suggest that an organisation is likely to encounter a number of concerns and problems at the operational management level, the main issues being the following:

- *Performance specification:*
  Early experience with environmental management systems has indicated that inadequate performance specifications, both with the system itself and with these that form part of the job description of individuals, are all too apparent. This is certainly borne out from the early experiences with quality systems implementation. Activities may not be well focused to organisational need in the short term and often only time with the system will solve this as operational management becomes more experienced in its use. Directive management must specify quite unambiguously to operational management just what is expected in terms of systems and individual performance. Frequently, performance is left to subjective interpretation which is tantamount to chance, whereas performance levels should be quantified and specified where wholly appropriate and possible to do so.

- *Information flow and content:*
  It is generally true that the quality of information flow and content can be extremely variable in systems applications, particularly where a new system is being developed and implemented. Information can be untimely, incomplete or poorly conceived and delivered. Perhaps the most important aspect identified in the development and implementation of environmental management systems is the inappropriate level of information passed through the system. Information flow and content should be commensurate with the ability and needs of the operation and it was frequently seen that information passing in the system was sometimes inadequately detailed for the task and at other times over-detailed. Likewise information flow could be too slow or conversely too rapid to comprehend in the context of system aims.

- *Excessive paperwork:*
  Operational management, more than any other management level, fear the notion that organisational implementation is a generator of excessive paperwork under which they will be swamped. Research has also indicated that where such fears were held at the systems initiation stage, that these are soon waylaid during implementation and that the system is not really a generator of the paperwork imagined although some aspects do hold store on the systematic recording, storage and retrieval of system aspects. If the environmental management system, like any other system, is appropriately conceived and administered there should

never be the need for excessive paperwork, just appropriate paperwork to do the job functionally and effectively.

- *Control mechanisms:*
  Control mechanisms are highlighted as a potential early environmental system problem but this is due essentially not to a lack of control but to the understanding of the change necessary in control methods. Most organisations naturally adopt a pattern of retrospective control revolving around the conceptual process of problem identification and remedy. Environmental management systems demand a pro-active and dynamic control mechanism to anticipate problems that may occur so that if they do the organisation can 'manage' the problem speedily and effectively.

- *System flow:*
  Operational management are likely in the early development of all systems to see the system as a one-way flow of practices and instructions which they respond to in the natural process of making the system work on a day-to-day basis. An essential aspect of environmental management systems is the necessity of feedback through the system making the system a two-way flow of information and feedback or a cycle of information. Only with the cyclic flow can the system self-perpetuate and develop and evolve to improve itself with time. The organisational ethos must be such that operational management sees themselves as part of the cycle of managing the holistic system, and not merely the hands-on part.

- *Review and audit:*
  For a variety of reasons, operational management do not always appreciate the part that they play in systems auditing and review. Auditing and review, emanating from operational management levels, is one of the frequently occurring problems seen in system implementation, usually quite simply because personnel do not know what audit and review entails, how it fits into the system and what their part is in its activity. Although audit and review falls within the remit of strategic and directive management levels, it should be remembered that audit and review is concerned with the operation of the environmental management system, with responsibilities for ensuring that standards are maintained and through use that constant improvement is made. This essentially rests with management at all levels but is particularly significant at operational level since most of the information needed to achieve review is generated from systems at operational level.

Managing the concerns and problems identified

Section 4.8, which follows, presents an overview and summary of environmental management systems development and implementation in which the key points that must be considered are highlighted in the form of a management checklist. Addressing these main points in the formulation of an environmental management system, some of the concerns and problems highlighted may be minimised or alleviated.

4.8   Environmental management systems: summary and overview

Summary of main issues

Chapter 4 has postulated an outline framework for developing an environmental management system within the organisation. To conclude both this chapter and Part B – Environmental Management: Systems Development, it may be appropriate to highlight the main issues identified. These are as follows:

- Changes in environmental legislation, environmentally driven market forces and increasing environmental expectations means that most organisations simply cannot afford to ignore environmental issues.
- To assume a pro-active stance to meet increasingly stringent environmental demands, organisations must adopt a structured approach to environmental management.
- Environmental management should be structured within an authoritative and recognised management framework, i.e. environmental management to the specification of BS 7750.
- A 'systems' approach is identified as the most appropriate route to pursuing environmental management.
- Preparatory environmental review is identified as the most significant determinant of successful environmental management as it lays the foundation of organisational philosophy and thinking.
- An environmental management system encompasses a great many organisational aspects and therefore it should take a holistic view of the entire organisation.
- Environmental management systems should be based fundamentally upon the management structure of the organisation and developed and implemented through three levels: strategic, directive and operational management.
- A key appointment in the formulation of an environmental management system is that of the environmental manager (environmental representative in BS 7750) to assume direct responsibility for the environmental management system.
- Environmental management must be the commitment, and be seen to be the commitment, of the organisation and emanate from the highest levels of management – 'top down' management is fundamental and essential, bottom driven systems will not be successful.

- The two key early determinants of successful environmental management formulation are clear and focused organisational policies and an unambiguous environmental statement as these form the basis for environmental standards, programmes and procedures.
- The centrepiece of an environmental management system is the environmental management manual which describes the procedures for implementing the environmental policy.
- The environmental management system manual must be available to all personnel involved with the system within the organisation and should describe their roles and responsibilities for the system.
- Information contained in the environmental manual should be pertinent, relevant and ostensibly simple, to facilitate ease of implementation. It is all too easy to over-write the manual. Information should be tiered and assisted by diagrammatic aids where appropriate.
- Environmental management systems should be developed with respect to current standards, those specified by BS 7750, regulatory bodies and applicable legislation.
- Education and training is essential to environmental management system development and implementation and is applicable at all managerial and operative levels.
- Monitoring and auditing are prerequisites to successful implementation but it should be noted that these activities check the system and not the work outputs.
- Provision of feedback should be a structured part of the system to ensure the cyclic flow of information and continuous systems improvement.
- An environmental management system may be developed around the core of an organisation's existing management system, such as a quality system meeting the requirements of BS 5750, providing it is suitably adapted to meet BS 7750.
- An organisation will, undoubtedly, encounter a great many difficulties and problems when developing and implementing an environmental management system. These are detailed in section 4.7. Whilst some are avoidable, it should be recognised that others are inevitable in a system approach and must be actively managed.

Overview

It is clear that a systems approach is a prerequisite to effective and efficient environmental management and that the development and implementation of an environmental management system is a time-consuming and complex initiative. Operation of a well-formulated environmental management system is, however, not the end of the task, but merely the beginning. For an environmental management system to be effective it must be maintained and improved over time and therefore organisational commitment to the system must be long-term. All levels of management and the personnel that operate the system on a day-to-day basis must aim for improvement and be fully aware that environmental management is an evolutionary process that demands continuous awareness, change and development. Although developing and implementing an environmental management system will be a daunting proposition and one that is likely to be undertaken in small steps and in discrete sections within the organisation, the longer-term objectives should be to encompass all organisational activities within a broader system and for this reason, if no other, the environmental management system should be perceived from a holistic perspective. This is essential, not simply because an organisation should be viewed as a whole, but because the organisation itself exists in an environment in which many changing variables exist. The organisation's environmental management system is but a smaller system within a much larger system, that of its environment, that very environment it seeks to protect.

References

1   British Standards Institution (BSI), BS 7750: *Specification for Environmental Management Systems* (1992).
2   British Standards Institution (BSI), BS 7229: *Guide to Quality Systems Auditing* (1991).
3   British Standards Institution (BSI), BS 5750: *Quality Systems (1979, revised 1987)*.

Part C:
Application of Environmental Management within the Construction Industry

5 Environmental Management in the Construction Process

5.1 The need for environmental management and environmental management systems in construction

Environmental management: a matter of attitude

Much has been banded about in recent years as to how ecology must be balanced with the man-made environment in an attempt to reintroduce traditional virtues of sustainable architecture. Given the problems that currently face the environment at local, national and international levels, not forgetting the global issues, the broader perspective is both valid and admirable and yet a holistic approach re-establishing building and construction within the laws of nature seems almost intangible at this time.

Manipulation of the environment in nearly all forms means that the construction industry invariably overrides nature rather than interpreting and symbiotically balancing itself with nature. It may be argued that some strides have been made in the environmental management of construction through eco-architecture and eco-engineering but, in the main, the construction industry is driven by financial determinants that, more often that not, preclude environmentally sound solutions being avidly sought. Ecologically sound buildings and structures are, of course, technically achievable and may, in fact, be more economic to construct, run and maintain than traditional solutions. They can use sustainable or man-made materials, be designed to use minimal and renewable energy and be developed on existing rather than new construction sites. Whilst a few developments have demonstrated such empathy, they are but a few. For any marked effect to be manifest, a radical shift in attitude within the construction industry would have to prevail, one that at national, international and global levels sought to rediscover the laws of nature and develop the environment within these constraints. Such a proposition would be years away if a valid proposition at all.

To a more restricted and perhaps realistic focus, environmentally managed construction can be addressed and is being addressed within the construction industry itself. Again however, practical environmental management necessitates a considerable change in perspective, attitude, procedures and practices if limited success is to be repeated and more widely perpetuated. Somewhat at its periphery, the construction industry has recognised the concept of 'green' or eco-construction and limited explorations could be

developed to provide a useful vehicle for the wider perpetuation of environmental management.

In practical terms, green or 'eco-construction' should have the following
broad aim:

> *To devise new methods or adapt existing methods of undertaking the 'total'*
> *construction process with greater empathy for the surrounding environment.*

This, of course, means that development studies, procurement, design and
construction should all be conducted within a framework of environmental
management. Moreover, it means that each contributor to the total construction process: lead consultant; main contractor; sub-contractors; suppliers; and other inputs should all operate an environmental management
system within their organisation to ensure their environmentally sympathetic contributions to the construction process. This is obviously idealistic
but unless environmental management is pursued across the board, only
isolated and minimum success will be achievable and the vast majority of
construction industry will trundle on regardless.

It is recognised that inroads have been made to the limited adoption of
environmental management concepts in the form of environmental assessments of some developments, some eco-architecture and through the marketing of some ecologically sound 'green' materials but little has been done to
make the construction process on site more environmentally secure and
certainly, in the main, little has been done as yet to address environmental
effects across the total construction process, an aspect with which other
industries have already had to come to terms.

Change will take place in these respects, however, quite simply because
organisations in all construction sectors will have to comply with increasing
vigour to changing perspectives, attitudes, procedures, market forces and,
more importantly, more stringent legislation, particularly regulations emanating from EC Directives that now affect all business activities including construction industry to a great extent. Some organisations have already
recognised this necessity in particular sectors and areas of construction
industry but the wider implications of environmental management are gra-
dually becoming more recognised across the industry even though some
early scepticism and resentment that hindered the widespread recognition
of quality assurance may exist at this time. In addition, interest in environmental management is necessary, particularly since construction industry is
gaining a somewhat infamous reputation for promulgating severely adverse
effects upon the environment both directly from its own activities and
indirectly from industry it supports through its resource demands. Regulation, which the construction industry simply cannot ignore, will be addressing
these effects more stringently in the future as the international trend towards
formal environmental management increases.

It has already been seen that profound change in attitudes and practices have taken place in many industrial and manufacturing sectors of the business world as a direct result of the increasing trend towards environmental protection. Change in business activity has mirrored the social change in attitude towards the way in which people perceive and want to safeguard their environments. Following this trend, construction industry, like manufacturing and industrialised businesses, is under considerable and increasing market and legislative pressure to improve the standards of its environmental performance, not just in specific aspects but across the total construction process.

For an industry that is recognised as developing and adapting reasonably readily to technological change but accepted as not being so receptive to procedural and managerial change, it is perhaps quite remarkable that the construction industry, despite its early apprehension, became significantly involved in quality assurance and quality management systems in the late 1980s. This one concession has demonstrated an attitude of change within the construction industry and one which is now more ready to consider and value the contribution that a concept such as environmental management can make.

An organisation that adopts environmental management and an environmental management system to the specification of BS 7750 will be well placed to both recognise and address the wind of change within the industry supporting the environment. Also this organisation will be able to play a significant part in the framework and structure for environmental management within which the construction industry is developing quite speedily.

Environmental management: its importance in construction

The construction industry has an unequivocal and considerable effect upon the environment: directly, since most development invariably means extensive environmental effects at the project workplace; indirectly, since most services and products used in the construction process consume resources, many of which are non-renewable, or in the case of products some may contribute to adverse environmental effects during their manufacture.

The single largest end product of the construction industry, buildings, greatly affect the environment since they use around two-thirds of all energy used. In addition, the construction of new buildings accounts for around 5 per cent of total energy consumption during their production processes. Not only this but buildings in use and the construction of buildings consume vast quantities of natural resources and are responsible most significantly for many undesirable environmental effects. The construction industry and effects upon the environment are, therefore, synonymous.

Environmental management in the construction industry is an extensive and thought provoking proposition. In an exploded view, environmental management must be approached from a range of directions to gain a comprehensive and accurate perspective of all the issues. This is true for a number of reasons. First, because the environment is directly and greatly affected by any construction project at its siting, environmental management must carefully consider the implications of the project on the environment at source and before any permission to develop is considered. Whilst nearly all construction is controlled through national and local legislative planning and consent procedures and has been for many years, European Community Directives announced in 1988 legislatively formalised the structure and detailed procedure of ensuring that the likely effects of specific new development on the environment are fully explored, understood and taken into account before any development decision is taken. This aspect of environmental management is termed *Environmental Assessment* (EA) and represents an environmental audit of a proposal, development or project. This aspect of environmental management falls within the remit of the developer or client and as actioned through the role of the lead consultant in association with specialist consultants.

Second, environmental management must become an inherent part of the organisation of those many and diverse contributors to the construction process; products materials and component suppliers; contractors; and other service inputs. The magnitude of the industry, the large number of inputs and the range of diversity of the people and processes involved gives construction much greater complexity than manufacturing and industrialised oriented businesses. This makes the implementation of environmental management so much more difficult. Companies should undertake a comprehensive environmental review to assess the effects that their activities, whether their outputs are products or services, have on the environment and make improvement where necessary to mitigate potentially adverse effects. It has been identified that tangible benefits can be accrued both within and outside the organisation through environmental management and the use of environmental management systems. Expectation of more stringent legislation in the future means that organisations, in particular those in the services and supply sectors of construction, must have a greater awareness of and challenge the requirements for environmental management. In this way they will be better placed to accommodate environmental auditing of their businesses, this also becoming an increasing demand in many commercial sectors.

Third and perhaps the most challenging aspect of the broader issues of environmental management is the implementation of environmental management throughout the construction process. At present it would be difficult to establish a clear line of environmental management from environmental assessment to environmental management on a project site. The total construction process assumes, probably quite wrongly, that all environmental effects have been fully and carefully considered in the environmental assessment, that green design opportunities have been grasped, that environmentally sympathetic products have been resourced and that the project site team will adopt environmentally sensitive practices. The chances of all these beneficial practices coming together across one project, particularly in view of the way that construction is structured, is currently most unlikely but in the future should become a laudable challenge. Specific EC directives are bringing more stringent regulations to particular aspects of construction works on site, for example, emission and discharge regulations and temporary workplace regulations. Environmentally minded contracting organisations will be better placed to meet such more rigorous regulations.

Returning to the general issues at this stage, however, there is little doubt that even within the construction industry there is an increasing concern for environmental protection and improved environmental performance of most organisations. Concern, expectations and legislation look set to become more stringent, and as such, organisations within all sectors of construction must become more aware of the need to assess the effects of their business on the environment. This is true in terms of the specific and broader aspects of environmental management. The most appropriate way in which organisations, of all kinds, can meet these demands is to consider the implementation of an environmental management system. Should environmental management become as prominent in the future as quality assurance systems have become, then the link between environmental assessment of construction development and environmental management of the contributing inputs will be firmly established, perhaps in the form of environmentally pre-qualifying both the project and the contributing participants. In the same way that BS 5750 quality systems assumed prominence in the mid-1980s, so BS 7750: Specification for Environmental Management Systems promises to have a major impact on the construction industry into the next century.

The environmental effects of construction

Since the construction industry holds such a great propensity to affect the environment, perhaps more so than other industries, frequently in beneficial ways, but often in the most detrimental and damaging ways, environmental management is simply prerequisite to its future constitution. The position of the construction industry within the environmental debate is central and vital to any attitude of change, since construction, in its constitution and processes, is a major contributor to environmental effects. Obviously, construction is a man-made process, but through time it has increasingly moved away from ecological symbiosis to establish the current eco-imbalance where natural resources in all forms have either become depleted or are subjected to continued adverse effects.

Some aspects of construction industry that give rise to adversarial effects are major and therefore instantly recognisable, but others are more muted and yet they are equally as damaging in their own way. The major effects of the construction industry upon the environment may be grouped within the following headings (see Figure 5.1).

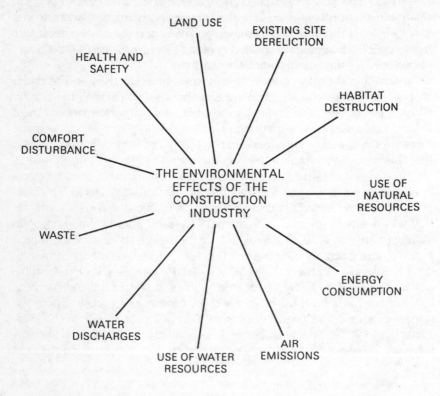

Figure 5.1   The main environmental effects of construction industry

- Land use.
- Existing site dereliction.
- Habitat destruction.
- Use of natural resources.
- Energy consumption.
- Air emissions.
- Use of water resources.
- Water discharges.
- Waste.
- Comfort disturbance.
- Health and safety.

Land use

Land use is perhaps the greatest environmental effect of construction industry. Construction projects invariably occupy land, consume space above land, utilise areas below land surface and propagate a host of effects acting directly and indirectly on the surrounding environment. The use of land for construction development is controlled under the physical planning regulations managed by local authorities. Within these regulations are the requirements for environmental assessment (EA) which exists to safeguard the use of land for developmental purposes and consider the potential effects upon the environmental of development before consent to develop is granted. This requirement stems directly from EC Directive 85/337/EEC[1] which came into force in 1988 and is now one of the most significant EC environmental oriented laws affecting construction industry activity.

Existing site dereliction

An unfortunate consequence of construction industry is the prevalence of developers who favour the use of new green field sites. Whilst this is understandable in the context of ease of development and cost effectiveness, the effect upon the environment is simply one of leaving existing buildings, structures and sites in derelict and ruinous condition. The situation is not helped by a tendency towards encouraging out of town shopping centres, urban retail centres, industrial estates, manufacturing parks and business parks which whilst making facilities available to a wider range and number of people does so at the expense of inner city renewal. Again, evaluation and control of such development forms an intrinsic aspect of EC, national and local legislation under EC Directive 85/337/EEC.

Habitat destruction

There is no doubt whatsoever that habitat destruction lies at the root of much vehement public condemnation of construction. Whilst planning regulations seek to consider the environmental effects of construction development on balance with the need for development and progress, a number of very high profile UK planning applications referred to national government level[2,3] have been on the side of development. Subsequent construction has, of course, taken its toll on natural amenities, landscape and wildlife and it is the often wasteful disregard for conservation which promotes such great hostility in public perception.

Use of natural resources

In addition to land use, the construction industry is well recognised for its utilisation of natural resources. Environmental effects from the use of such resources are both direct and indirect. Deforestation is a direct environmental effect from the use of natural timber products for example. Quarrying is another direct effect of using natural stone and aggregates within the construction processes with environmental effect resulting from the retrieval processes. Indirect environmental effects result from manufactured materials, components and products that affect the environment adversely during their production processes.

Energy consumption

It is recognised that around two-thirds of all energy consumption in the UK is attributable to the construction of buildings or the use and servicing of buildings.[4] Much of the energy is invariably wasted but, moreover, the natural resources, for example fossil fuels, are even more depleted and for little reason. It is interesting that the Department of Energy[5] suggested some years ago that there is the technical potential to meet around half of the current UK energy demand through renewable rather than expendable sources.

Air emissions

One may not necessarily think of construction industry and air emission as greatly synonymous although the use of construction plant and equipment will frequently give rise to some atmospheric pollutants such as diesel fumes, whilst some construction operations give off smoke and other airborne toxic wastes. If, however, one thinks of chlorofluorocarbons (CFCs) and similar gaseous emissions then the environmental effect is overwhelming. As an indication of the seriousness of air emission, around half of the CFC emissions emanate from buildings in some form, for example, from insulation material, refrigerants, and fire extinguishing mediums. The global environmental effect on the ozone layer resulting from such emissions is well recognised and construction industry is heavily to blame, again from its activities both direct and indirect.

Use of water resources

The construction industry both directly and indirectly consumes vast water resources although this is not in itself a problem of environmental effect. The end-products buildings, however, do give rise to environmental effects through the need for water and sewage treatment plants, water supply and storage facilities and the environmental effects associated with supplying and maintaining water resources to new and developing infrastructures. These lead, of course, to the knock-on effects of development which demand new developments and therefore ultimately perpetuate their own cycle of demand for greater water resources.

Water discharges

Environmental effects from construction industry are apparent, again from direct and indirect activities. At the direct level, environmental effects can result from inappropriate construction site practices that discharge pollutants, for example oil waste into water courses or indirectly through contaminants that go into land that feed into natural water sources. Two recent cases, one inadvertent and one admitted case of oil spillage, reflected this commonly occurring aspect of construction site activity.

Waste

Waste emanating from construction industry is a major problem leading to detrimental environmental effects. In the UK for example, an estimated total of 400 million tonnes of waste is created annually.[6] Whilst over a quarter is controlled waste, the remainder is a result of particular commercial, industrial mining and agricultural activities in addition to domestic waste practices. Around 8 per cent of all waste results from construction demolition which due to inadequate grading is not recycled but deposited in land-fill dumps. Approximately a quarter of all waste results from mining and quarrying, an undetermined amount of which arises from the provision of raw materials used in the construction processes. A further 17 per cent, approximately, results from industrial waste, a proportion of which arises in the production processes of materials and products used in the construction processes. There is little doubt that waste management is a key consideration for construction industry to address.

Comfort disturbance

Environmental effects of construction result in a number of comfort disturbances to individuals living and working in the environs surrounding any construction project. These are well recognised and include:

- Noise (of construction operations and equipment).
- Dust (from processes and traffic).
- Nuisance (e.g. temporary dwellings, construction traffic).
- Hazardous contamination (e.g. toxic wastes).
- Other visual disturbances (signs, advertising boards, etc.).

Health and safety

An obvious environmental effect of the construction process is that its activities carry an inherent level of danger to both employees and the public. EC directives have brought stringent regulations in two areas:

(i) Health and safety to public in the general environment.
(ii) Health and safety in the workplace.

Both are significant to the construction process since construction projects are:

- Temporary workplaces (subject to EC directives on temporary workplace activity) and involve the health and safety of employees.
- Workplaces that affect the surrounding environment and have an effect on the public.

Mitigating the environmental effects of construction through environmental management

The promotion and success of environmental management in mitigating the effects of construction in the future will be fundamentally determined by two major influences:

(i) Legislation (both current and future): standards for environmental management at project level and organisational level (i.e. of the participants) must be appropriate to need and procedures in order to ensure compliance with the standards.
(ii) Commitment: to environmental management by employers (developers/clients) and all those organisations who participate in the construction process.

Environmental management must address the environmental effects of construction at regulatory, organisational and project levels. Measures to do this include:

- *Environmental Assessment:* the process of assessment by a developer of the potential environmental effects of a proposed development and subsequently considered by the planning authority in deciding whether to grant planning permission. In addition to the imposed legislative requirements, some employers are using environmental assessment as a medium for operational organisation and therefore the concepts are being applied outside those criteria of legislation, i.e. application on a voluntary basis.
- *Environmental Management:* the contribution to the construction process of environmentally managed organisations (product suppliers and services) through the implementation of environmental management systems within their organisations. Although initiatives are voluntary, legislation in specific areas, e.g. production processes of products, is placing more stringent demands upon organisations to follow an environmental policy.
- *Environmental Surveys and Environmental Site Practice:* the detailed evaluation of the construction project to determine the optimum envir-

onmentally sound construction practices. An imposing aspect in this area is the new EC Directives on safety in the workplace for example, and amended national legislation in health and safety.

Whilst some of the aspects mentioned, for example health and safety in construction, are issues of such magnitude that they merit and are subject to written works in their own right, they form an important part of the concept of environmental management in construction and will be addressed, in context, subsequently.

The importance of environmental management systems in construction

Environmental management systems are fundamental and essential to the demonstration of environmental management. An environmental management system creates the necessary framework and structure within an organisation to ensure that its activities meet with current environmental legislation and that the environmental effects of its business, in all their forms, are recognised and actively managed. It was identified in Chapter 1 that an environmental management system is important to an organisation, not simply because it provides continuity and uniformity of environmental response, but because it enables the organisation to engender an environmental ethos within which policies, objectives and goals are formed and procedures and instructions carried out. It provides a basis for the socio-technical and management structure within the organisation to meet any environmental challenge.

In the early part of Chapter 3 the main priorities of an environmental management system were identified. Of these priorities, all of which are extremely important to the formulation of an environmental management system, one stands out as vitally important, that of 'meeting current and future environmental legislation'. This is particularly pertinent to the construction industry. With rapidly developing EC legislation the construction industry invariably finds itself in a state of flux. Difficulties in harmonising practices across the EC, disparities in standards and variations in statutory legislation make it difficult for any organisation to keep abreast of its environmental responsibilities. The pro-active stance of an environmental management system enables an organisation within the construction industry, in fact any industry for that matter, to maintain active and on-going awareness of its environmental situation and manage it accordingly. Moreover, it places the organisation in the advantageous position of being able to respond more easily and quickly to changes in its environmental situation, for example changes in legislation or market forces.

Until recent times, any formal application of environmental management within the construction industry had been limited ostensibly to a relatively small number of construction projects with high value and with high environmental risk. These have been predominantly in the petrochemicals, power and waste management industries, highways and civil engineering and large building developments. Such instances have seen environmental assessments of potential development required by legislation, but also environmental management systems implemented by larger manufacturing and industrial organisations. Environmental management systems are seen by such organisations as a necessity in meeting both the internal and external demands placed upon them. Environmental management systems are important to larger organisations, particularly those who act in the capacity of developers or clients, and equally important to consultants, contractors, sub-contractors and suppliers who serve such clients. All resource inputs to the total construction process have an important part to play in the environmental management framework and environmental management systems are the ideal mechanism to ensure that the optimum contribution is made. This is emphasised further in recent EC Directives and statutory legislation that places considerable and clear obligations for environmental management upon developers, clients, designers, contractors and suppliers. In meeting these commitments in the longer term, environmental management systems will be a certain necessity to many of these organisations.

Environmental management systems are essential to:

- Developers and client organisations: who should ensure the environmental efficacy of the projects they develop and procure.
- Design consultants: who should ensure design considerations are compatible with environmental needs.
- Contractors: who should ensure environmental management of the project at the workplace and within its surrounding environs.
- Suppliers: who should ensure the environmental soundness of their materials, components and products used in the construction process during manufacture and delivery.

5.2   Environmental management and environmental management systems in construction

Large organisations (developers/clients)

Early environmental management systems have emerged in larger organisations, in particular those at the forefront of manufacturing, power and the petrochemical industries. Such organisations represent among their many nationwide and often multi-national activities some of the largest clients of the construction industry. Large construction clients tend, in the main, to be diverse, sophisticated and are, because of the nature of their core business, most environmentally aware. These organisations will create environmental effects from their business and will be well aware of them, quite simply because they will have to meet some of the most stringent environmental and health and safety regulations within any commercial business sector. In addition, most large organisations of this type will be subject to rigorous policing by external regulatory bodies and are likely to undergo frequent audit. Such organisations will demonstrate corporate commitment to the environment, will implement a comprehensive environmental management system and, in so doing, will accrue the benefits of environmental management. The major implication for the construction industry is that such organisations will expect their consultants, contractors and suppliers to be equally committed to environmental management.

Smaller organisations (developers/clients)

Smaller organisations who act in the capacity of developer or clients to the construction industry may not be quite as advanced in the development and implementation of environmental management as the larger organisations, but will certainly be aware of its demands in the commercial workplace. Whilst many will not be completely familiar with standards for formal environmental management systems they are likely to have addressed systems organisation through their support to quality management initiatives. Such organisations are likely therefore to adapt their existing quality management system to take account of the increasing requirements for environmental management. Again, as an intrinsic part of meeting environmental management, these organisations will expect those organisations serving their requirements to be environmentally aware.

Consulting organisations

Construction consultants, in particular those in the design sector, are coming under increasing pressure to mitigate many of the potential environmental effects of their designs. Whilst most design practices will not have embarked upon the formal road to environmental management systems within their own organisations, many will no doubt be aware of their increasing responsibilities and obligations to environmental management of construction projects through the demands of their clients. New legislation in health and safety, for example, is requiring not only clients but also their design consultants to assume a more prominent role and accept greater responsibility throughout the construction project.

Contracting organisations

Main contractors and sub-contractors are at the forefront of environmental management at project level. The vast majority of environmental effects are recognised at this level, at the project site itself and in its environs. Minimising environmental effects in all their forms must be the first priority for the contractor. This is taken in the broadest context to include not only the environmental issues in land use, but also in protection of people, both employees and the public, in use of resources and in the minimisation of other disturbances to the project environs. A structured approach to such obligations is essential and environmental management systems exist to meet this challenge.

Supply organisations

The production of materials and components used within the construction processes are marshalled to a much greater extent than other resource inputs to construction, simply because they represent manufactured products and environmental management is often an intrinsic aspect of their production processes. In general, there is little doubt that this sector will come under even closer scrutiny in the future as the demand for 'green' products increases and as industry moves towards the eco-labelling of goods and products. For those suppliers who do not currently pursue environmental management, they are likely to find that in the future environmental management systems will become a necessity in meeting such requirements.

The environmentally managed organisation

An environmentally managed organisation is essentially one that operates and maintains an environmental management system to the specifications of BS 7750 (see Figure 5.2). Any organisation within construction implementing such a system is in an advantageous position over one that does not. Benefits are potentially available to such an organisation and these are felt both within and external to the organisation.

A construction organisation committed to an environmental management system will be in an advantageous position to meet the requirements for:

- Mitigating the severe environmental effects of construction projects.
- Increasingly stringent environmental legislation within construction both nationally and internationally.
- More rigorous health, safety and welfare regulations on construction projects, nationally and internationally.
- Closer control of environmental effects from construction activities, both on the site and in the surrounding environs.
- Pre-qualification, should clients demand environmental management as a basis for short-listing or appointment.

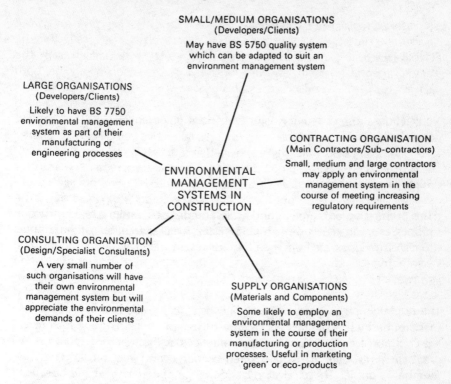

SMALL/MEDIUM ORGANISATIONS
(Developers/Clients)

May have BS 5750 quality system
which can be adapted to suit an
environment management system

LARGE ORGANISATIONS
(Developers/Clients)

Likely to have BS 7750
environmental management
system as part of their
manufacturing or
engineering processes

ENVIRONMENTAL
MANAGEMENT
SYSTEMS IN
CONSTRUCTION

CONTRACTING ORGANISATION
(Main Contractors/Sub-contractors)

Small, medium and large contractors
may apply an environmental
management system in the
course of meeting increasing
regulatory requirements

CONSULTING ORGANISATION
(Design/Specialist Consultants)

A very small number of
such organisations will have
their own environmental
management system but will
appreciate the environmental
demands of their clients

SUPPLY ORGANISATIONS
(Materials and Components)

Some likely to employ an
environmental management
system in the course of their
manufacturing or production
processes. Useful in marketing
'green' or eco-products

Figure 5.2   Environmental management systems within the construction process

- European and international operations and expansion, where environmental management may be more prominent than in the organisation's home market.
- More rigorous testing and approval of construction products within a framework of 'green' policies (eco-labelling).

Awareness of responsibilities

To be in a pro-active management position to accrue these potential advantages a construction organisation must be aware of and address the following requirements:

(i)   EC Directives and how these impinge upon construction.
(ii) EC Standards and how these evolve from Directives.
(iii) How (i) and (ii) above translate into national regulations and standards.

Sections 5.3 and 5.4 present the EC legislative framework and the legal framework for environmental management in construction.

5.3   The EC legislative framework

EC Directives

Background

EC Directives are, in essence, laws which the governments of the member countries uphold through their own national legislative frameworks. Until the mid-1980s, Directives were highly specified and detailed, and as a result they could take a considerable time both to develop and be agreed upon among the various member councils. To address this issue, EC Ministers agreed to develop Directives based upon essential requirements, supported by standards. These standards are drafted by the European Committee for Standardisation (CEN) and the European Committee for Electrotechnical Standards (CENELEC), by mandate from the EC Commission.

Purpose

The fundamental purpose of EC Directives is to provide freedom of movement for business resources, goods and services by developing and maintaining common standards and business practices across member countries. A great many EC Directives have been proffered and adopted among the member countries. These envelop a wide range of commercial and business interests, some of which impinge upon the construction industry both directly and indirectly. In recent years, the main focus of interest for the construction industry has been the gradual dissolution of trading barriers with freedom of movement to products and services proliferating, whilst in the future EC Directives in specialised areas, such as environmental management, look set to impart increasingly rigorous demands on the construction industry.

Difficulties of development and implementation

Given the purpose of EC Directives, to assist trading between member countries, perhaps the greatest difficulty in developing and implementing directives is in the requirement to accommodate the considerable diversity in culture, legislation, procedures and practices that exist across member countries. Directives meet with the unenviable task of striking a fair balance between the need to open up trade frontiers whilst protecting the national interests of the member countries. To achieve this, Directives provide the broad legislative requirements from which member countries develop their own national, regional and local legislation. In this way, the desired level of harmonisation is achieved whilst retaining the national characteristics of each member country.

Construction industry directives

EC Directives are many and varied with some Directives affecting the construction industry in a direct way whilst others impart their influence somewhat indirectly. Some Directives developed many years ago have been adopted whilst others are still in their evolutionary stages for subsequent introduction at some time in the future. In an attempt to simplify the current status of EC Directives, it may be said that Directives affecting the activities of the construction industry may be broadly grouped into a number of distinct categories. These are as follows:

- Professional practices.
- Construction design (includes elements of construction management).
- Construction products.

Professional practices

This group of EC Directives encompasses such aspects as procurement form and tendering procedures in the public and utility services sectors. These Directives provide for competitive procurement on a non-discriminatory basis across member countries, provide a unified mechanism for redress in the event of contractual difficulty and lay the ground rules for conciliation procedures. Other specific Directives in this group cover some private sector works where subsidies from public funds are involved, matters of liability and insurance and also the common recognition of professional construction qualifications.

Construction design

Whilst it is true to say that very few Directives actually envelop procedures and practices in the design sector of construction industry, a considerable number of Directives relate to what might be considered to be construction industry and environmental management matters, although specific aspects of these affect the roles and responsibilities of clients and designers in addition to contractors. Among the many and again varied EC Directives, four categories are important in the context of this review. These are:

(i) *The Eco-Management and Auditing Scheme*: essentially an environmental protection system.
(ii) *The Environmental Assessment Directive*: detailed analysis of the environmental implications of a proposed development project.
(iii) *The EC Framework Directive: Health and Safety*: a set of supporting Directives concerning health, safety and welfare in and around the workplace.

(iv) *Register of Regulations (Environmental)*: numerous individual and associated Directives and regulations covering the environmental effects of procedures and practices of an organisation's activities.

These aspects are addressed in detail in subsequent sections and chapters.

Construction products

The Construction Products Directive is perhaps the most well known of Directives directly influencing construction industry. Adopted by member countries in the late 1980s, the Directive is designed to promote the uniform standard and acceptance of products within the EC. The Directive has two major effects upon products used in the construction industry. First, products marketed within the EC must meet the requirement of fitness for purpose, and second, where construction products are fit and meet with European technical specifications or standards the product may carry the *CE Mark* denoting approval. Whilst not all materials and products used in the construction process will conform to the requirement of the Construction Products Directive currently, certainly in the future the requirements of other Directives will determine that they should. It is the Directives, therefore, that will place increasingly stringent requirements upon the construction process in the future. Products Directives are supported by standards, details of which follow subsequently. The standards of products used in construction, as with all products, must identify the products' intended use, conditions of use and provide details of performance where appropriate.

Of particular reference to environmental management is the EC Directive concerned with the eco-labelling of products. The eco-labelling initiative seeks to identify those products that are advantageous to environment protection. The environmental effects throughout the life-cycle of the product are considered and where a product is deemed to be environmentally friendly an eco-label may be awarded. Many such products are, of course, likely to be used within the construction industry and eco-labelling may, in the future, become an important aspect of material and product specification.

EC standards

Background

The EC legislative framework places a fundamental and important dependence upon standards to support Directives. Until the advent of the wider European Community, standards were ostensibly developed at a national level and applied internally to the activities of the country of origin. As one might imagine, such an approach led to tangential activity and disparate standard-making. A fundamental aim of EC legislation is to bring the practices of member countries in line and develop a framework of standards to support EC Directives.

The standardisation process

The European Committee for Standardisation (CEN), mentioned earlier, is charged with the responsibility of harmonising standards within the EC. CEN comprises the national standard-making bodies of the EC, and through their Technical Committees (TCs), with representatives from all member countries, they are responsible for all eco-standards impinging upon construction industry. These standards already comprise several thousand with more to follow in the future.

Product specification

A large programme of standardisation is currently under way within CEN and many of the standards nearing finalisation and to be adopted in the future are product specifications. These are, quite notably, important to the future of the construction industry. Base euro-codes are being developed to cover the design of structures in specific ways and these will be supported by new standards on materials and products.

The CE Mark

The CE Mark is used to indicate conformity to essential requirements specified by the Construction Products Directive and other applicable Directives as already outlined. Procurers and specifiers will, however, need to be aware of the significance of claims of conformity and use of such approval marks. An official CE mark must be supported by independent testing or certification and the user must be satisfied that the product does meet fitness for intended purpose.

The CE Mark indicates that a product meets a number of essential requirements set by the Construction Products Directive, a number of which are a part of meeting environmental performance criteria. These are:

- Energy, economy and heat retention.
- Health, hygiene and the environment.
- Mechanical resistance and stability.
- Protection against noise.
- Safety in use.
- Safety in case of fire.

The CE Mark consists of the letters CE, followed by the product manufacturer's name, a brief description of the product and any classification applicable, the inspection body approving the product and the certificate number.

The translation of EC Directives to national regulation and standards

When government ministers of the member countries of the EC adopt a Directive they undertake to implement that Directive within their own country and within their national legislative and regulating framework. In the UK for example, adopting a Directive may require an amended or new Act of Parliament being introduced supported by new or revised regulation. To illustrate such translation one can focus upon the Health and Safety group of Directives. In the UK, the Health and Safety Commission (HSC) is enforcing regulations, which together with the existing provisions of the Health and Safety at Work Act and The Building Regulations, will effectively implement the EC Directives. In addition, regulations may be supported by codes of practice and again the HSC is issuing approved codes as an aid to using the regulations. Each member country of the EC will develop and implement national legislation and regulation in the same way. This should lead to a uniform pattern of translation across the EC.

One of the major difficulties of such an endeavour is that EC legislation is currently, and will be for some years to come, in a state of development and change. This means that the whole area of Directives, standard-making, systems development and certification is in a state of flux. Any vagueness in these matters is not unintentional, as it would be most unwise to propound a situation as fact now, knowing full well that the situation may change in the near future.

What is more certain is that compromise has to be made in reaching legislative agreement across the member countries of the EC and already the generic European standards and regulations may not be as comprehensive or proficient as those of individual member countries. For example a euro-standard may not be as good as a British Standard. To alleviate any difficulty EC Directives merely state the essential requirements from which individual member states are free to develop their own standards as long as they meet the basic requirements. Where exceptional practice is demonstrated within a member country then this is filtered back to the European situation. A good example of this was BS 5750, essentially being adopted as the European standard for quality systems as EN 29000.

The importance of environmental management and environmental management systems to the legislative processes

The distinction between directives and standards is quite simple: a directive specifies the fundamental requirement whilst the standards specifies acts that allows the directive to be met. The requirement of a management system, of any kind, is that its implementation allows standards, and therefore directives, to be satisfied. An environmental management system, given its careful development and sound implementation, should allow an organisation to satisfy any environmental management set by an EC Directive, European or national regulation or standard. The environmental management system therefore, represents a perfect vehicle for the organisation to travel any environmental route desired irrespective of its orientation within the construction process.

5.4 The legislative framework for environmental management in construction

The EC Eco-Management and Auditing Scheme (CEMAS)

General

The EC Eco-Management and Auditing Scheme (CEMAS) will be of particular interest to organisations who seek to:

- Develop an environmental management system that conforms to European legislation.
- Expand or diversify their business operations into European and international commercial markets in the future.

Purpose

The basic premise of the Eco-Management and Auditing Scheme is to create a greater awareness of, and empathy for, environmental protection across the European Community. The scheme requires countries to develop and implement a structured eco-management and auditing process within their national regulating frameworks. Companies that participate in the scheme are required to develop and implement an *environmental protection system* with their organisation. This essentially involves the establishment of an environmental management system.

Status

In the UK for example, an environmental management system to the specification of BS 7750 satisfies the vast majority of the eco-requirements. The Eco-Management and Auditing Scheme does differ slightly in that it places a greater emphasis on audit as a function to be supported by detailed policy intention and public statements of environmental performance but such demands can be accommodated with a organisation's system quite readily.

Certainly in general, an organisation that establishes a BS 7750 environmental management system is well placed to meet both current and future demands of European and international environmental performance.

Requirements

Organisations that participate in the scheme must undertake the following:

- Develop, implement and maintain an environmental protection system (environmental management system).
- Analyse and review the environmental performance of their system.
- Issue public information on their environmental performance.
- Provide a public statement of their environmental performance, verified by an independent accredited environmental auditor.

Structure and constitution

The EC Eco-Management and Auditing Scheme is available to any organisation involved in industrial, production manufacturing, service and distributing businesses. In considering their business activities at a site or complex an organisation must satisfy a number of conditions based upon the above requirements, these being:

- To undertake a comprehensive environmental review of their business site or complex.
- Develop and implement an environmental protection system (environmental management system) based on environmental reviews.
- Make an environmental statement on their activities looking ahead to their future intentions.
- Ensure their statement is verified by an independent accredited environmental auditor.

In addition to the requirements of industrial organisations member countries are required to provide a national framework in which such schemes can operate. To meet the requirement, each member country must introduce an accreditation system for approving and certifying the accreditation of environmental auditors who under the EC Eco-Management and Auditing Scheme will audit the participating organisation. In the UK, for example, this process follows closely to that recognised in the field of quality assurance where the Department of Trade and Industry (DTI), through the National Accreditation Council for Certification Bodies (NACCB) accredit particular bodies to act as certifiers to participating organisations.

The importance of the Eco-Management and Auditing Scheme

The EC Eco-Management and Auditing Scheme has a number of strengths and prescribe a number of benefits to participating organisations. The strengths are that:

- The Scheme is EC-wide and therefore encourages uniformity across the Community.
- The Scheme has the full backing of each member country.
- The Scheme is likely, in the longer term, to achieve international accep- tance.
- The Scheme is bringing a new and wider awareness and appreciation of environmental issues which had hitherto been unrealised.

The potential benefits for participating organisations include:

- Recognition in a national, European and international system of environ- mental management.
- Use, where appropriate, of a Euro-wide registration logo.
- Listing in the EC Eco-Management and Auditing Scheme register of approved organisations.

Problems with the scheme

Without doubt the major difficulty facing the EC Eco-Management and Auditing Scheme in the early stages is its voluntary nature. In the same way that quality assurance schemes met with scepticism in its evolutionary process so too has environmental management.

A further issue is the Eco-Management and Auditing Scheme's preoccupa- tion with auditing activity which, whilst focusing on this very important aspect, appears to neglect the rather more fundamental issue of what needs to be audited and against what regulations and standards performance should be measured by. Certainly in the UK system, such aspects are well catered for in the specification for environmental management systems and should not prove too problematic to satisfy.

The future development of CEMAS

Whilst in its evolutionary stages CEMAS is essentially voluntary, the EC has declared that it sees the scheme becoming mandatory as organisations across many commercial sectors, including contracting, respond positively to developing a Euro-wide framework. There are early indications[7] that organisations are beginning to pledge support to the scheme, appreciating that there are benefits to be accrued from being ahead of commercial competition.

In the same way that quality assurance schemes have become almost prerequisite to organisations seeking work for larger private sector clients and public bodies, CEMAS is likely to become a pre-qualification criterion. Certainly, the EC has suggested that the scheme is EC-funded and many of these schemes already involve aspects of the construction industry.

The EC Environmental Assessment Directive

General

The EC Environmental Assessment Directive will be of particular interest to developers, clients, consultants, indeed any participant, to large-scale projects and major developments in many construction sectors.

The Directive, (85/337/EEC),[8] agreed to by member countries in 1985 and enacted in 1988, is without doubt the most significant piece of European legislation affecting environmental management within the construction process.

The concept of Environmental Assessment

Environmental Assessment (EA) is:

> *an appraisal technique for ensuring that the potential environmental effects of every new development are identified and considered before any approval is given.*

Environmental assessment, as a concept, has been incorporated into the planning and consent procedures of EC member countries to give effect to the Directive, although there is some disparity in implementation across member countries, as one might expect.

Environmental assessment

Environmental Assessment (EA), or Environmental Impact Assessment (EIA) as it is sometimes termed, is essentially the concept and process by which detailed information addressing the likely environmental effects of a development or project is gathered and evaluated by the developer or client organisation before being considered by the planning authority in deciding if planning permission should be formally granted. The collection of information documenting the project's potential environmental effects is the *environmental statement*.

Environmental statement

The environmental statement (ES) is a publicly available document submitted to the planning authority and it accompanies the developer's planning application. Generation of the environmental statement is the responsibility of the developer as is gathering all the information and facts needed for its development. In practice, it is likely that the developer will employ a consultant to conduct the detailed investigation and produce the statement.

The environmental statement may, depending upon circumstances, be brief and simple or lengthy and complex but it must provide a clear description of the project's likely environmental effects on a range of conventional environmental factors.[9]

Environmental assessment: scope of legislation

The initial decision by the developer as to whether a particular development proposal is subject to environmental assessment is crucial. To assist in this direction, the EC Directive lists the distinct categories of development:

- Annex I Projects: *These are projects for which an environmental assessment is required in every case.* Nine categories of project are encompassed and include, for example: power stations; chemical works; steel manufacturing; aerodromes; land-fill sites for specific waste products.
- Annex II Projects: *These are projects for which environmental assessment is required if the proposed project is likely to give rise to significant environmental effects.* Over eighty types of projects in eleven main classifications are included, for example: petroleum operations in the Extraction Industry; surface storage of natural gas in the Energy Industry; an urban development project in Infrastructure Projects.

Assessing a project's significance

The Directive allows EC member countries to use their discretion as to whether a project falls within the remit of Annex II projects. As different approaches are adopted in practice this can lead to a considerable lack of uniformity in selection procedures.

In assessing the significance of projects that fall into Annex II of the Directive, the following points should be considered:

- Is the project likely to give rise to particularly adverse environmental effects?
- Is the project to occupy a particularly sensitive location?
- Is the project of local or wider importance?

In the UK, for example, guidance on assessing the significance of Annex II projects is a matter for local authorities and this is perhaps appropriate since it is at local level rather than national or European level that the real considerations must be addressed.

A developer may decide that a proposed project comes within the remit of the Directive and within which Annex it is appropriately categorised, or alternatively the developer can refer the proposal to the planning authorities. In the latter case, a minimum amount of information must be available and in practice it is usually the case that the planning authority will decide that an environmental assessment is necessary when it receives the planning application from the developer.

Projects not subject to environmental assessment

Obviously, many projects are not encompassed within the Directive, yet still represent major developments which may give rise to significant environmental effects. When environmental assessment is not a precondition under the Directive, the environmental effects of the project will still be assessed by the planning authorities in making a decision as to whether or not to give formal permission for development.

A considerable number of organisations involved in procuring major projects use these principles and practices of environmental assessment, not to meet EC requirements, but more fundamentally to provide a structured approach to assessing the environmental effects of their proposed activities.

The problems encountered with the Environmental Assessment Directive

Perhaps the greatest single problem involves the wider acceptance of the concept of environmental assessment. By their nature, projects and developments subject to environmental assessment are likely to be somewhat sensitive, even controversial.[1,2] Disharmony between developer and the planning authorities, made all the more fraught by public intervention, can mean that the formal process of environmental assessment can take months, even years, where proposals are passed to government level for consultation and outcome.

Working within the EC Directive can also be somewhat problematic. The interpretation of the Directive into the various national legislative processes has shown some dysfunctionality and led to practice across member countries differing from that which was expected from the common interpretation of the Directive. Under the Treaty of Rome, the European Commission has a duty to ensure that Directives are fairly and uniformly interpreted and administered across member countries.

Interpretation can again become difficult if one looks at environmental factors, in particular the terms 'direct' and 'indirect' environmental effects. These categories, undefined within the Directive, can lead to considerable ambiguity when assessing the significance of a project and therefore interpretation relies upon careful judgement by the developer conducting the environmental assessment.

Benefits of the Environmental Assessment Directive

The benefits of the Environmental Assessment Directive to organisations are that:

- It provides the basis for better decision making in the procurement of their projects.
- It ensures that the potential environmental effects of their proposals are fully considered.
- It allows the formulation of projects within a framework of greater safeguard and acceptability.
- It promotes greater interaction between the developer and planning and approval authorities.
- It provides the judgemental processes to be administered more systematically, timely and effectively.

Public perception

A structured approach to environmental assessment under the EC Directive provides information and evaluation of the potential environmental effects of a development or project in terms that are perhaps more easily understood. This is fundamental to the concept, as an important part of processing any planning application is the interpretation of public feeling. Many projects are especially sensitive to public opinion, in particular where local environmental principles or issues are at stake. Environmental assessment can make the public better informed, and therefore any fear they hold can be relayed to the planning authority in sensible and constructive ways. It is a requirement that the environmental statement is written in non-technical language and this serves to better inform the lay-person. Most difficulties in environmental issues and the construction process arise from a fundamental failing to inform the public to an adequate degree.

The future development of environmental assessment

Environmental assessment as a concept and practice is mandatory within the scope of the Directive. Legislation is not static however, and it is likely that in the future some revisions may be made to the detail of the legislation – for example, increasing the range of project types covered. In addition, following the trend set in the Eco-Management and Auditing Scheme (CEMAS), more rigorous monitoring and verification procedures may come into effect to control development and land use more carefully. Certainly, there is little doubt that across EC member countries, construction industry is moving into a planning control system in which environmental management and environmental management systems will assume greater significance in the future.

The EC Framework Directive: health and safety legislation

General

The EC Framework Directive will be of particular interest to clients, consultants and contractors within the construction industry, since under this directive, regulation places considerable obligations upon all participants with regard to general health and safety matters.

The EC Framework Directive,[10] enacted in 1989, is supported by a number of individual Directives which have been in force since 1993. As a group these Directives form the structure for health and safety matters in and around the business and organisational workplace.

Like the EC Environmental Assessment Directive, the Framework Directive is one of the most significant pieces of European legislation affecting environmental management within the construction industry. It is all the more significant within the construction process since it views health and safety matters in a different context, placing onerous responsibility not just upon the contractor but also upon the client and his appointed consultants.

The Framework Directive

The principal aim of the Framework Directive is to create an awareness of, and respect for, the fundamental principles of health and safety in the workplace, to avoid unnecessary working risk and where this is not intrinsically possible then to minimise the risk as far as it is practicable to do so.

The health and safety directives

The general EC Framework Directive is supported by a group of Directives related to health and safety matters. A number of these have been in force across EC member countries since January 1993 whilst further Directives were enacted in January 1994. Those directly affecting construction industry are:

- The Workplace Directive.
- The Use of Work Equipment Directive.
- The Personal Protection Equipment Directive.
- The Manual Handling of Loads Directive.
- The Temporary Workers Directive.
- The Construction Sites Directive.

Other specific and subsidiary Directives concerning general safety of the employee's workplace include those relating to: use of computer displays; safety and health of pregnant workers; exposure to carcinogenic substances.

The accent of all these Directives is to essentially make the workplace and its environs a safe and healthy working environment, and in the case of construction, to provide a safe temporary work site for both employees and the neighbouring public.

Requirements of the Directives

The family of health and safety Directives are to some extent quite broad and general in content and as such they can be open to inappropriate interpretation. The general demands are to provide an environment that is healthy and safe, so far as is reasonably practical. This vagueness should however not be misinterpreted as weakness, since national legislation such as the UK's Management of Health and Safety at Work Regulations (1992),[11] for example, describe in some detail the specific requirements that are laid down in statutory legislation.

Whilst health and safety has always been a matter for the employer and the employee to a large extent, Directives now place greater emphasis upon suppliers of articles, equipment or materials used in the workplace to be safe and healthy to the working environment. This places a new emphasis upon the design aspect of construction and will be addressed subsequently.

Within the Directives and national legislation, an employer of more than five persons is required to prepare a *Safety Statement* based on a safety policy and plans which describe the manner in which employees are safeguarded from the general health and safety hazard at work. Whilst this may be quite straightforward for a factory situation, in temporary construction workplaces this could prove to be a daunting proposition.

Health and safety obligations

The construction industry is faced with a much greater challenge than other industries with regard to health and safety matters. The transient nature of a construction workforce makes the management of health and safety over a project and on a day-to-day basis difficult to maintain. It is well recognised that the risky nature of construction itself contributes significantly to the large number of injuries sustained, but most health and safety problems emanate from management failure to anticipate risk during not only the construction phase but the design stage. The EC Directives attempt to redress this deficiency by placing responsibility across the construction process.

National legislation developed from EC Directives has resulted in regulation which places the following obligations upon contractual parties:

The Client – must undertake the following:
• Appoint a planning supervisor.
• Appoint a principal contractor.
  Their function is to co-ordinate health and safety matters across the design and construction phases.
• Ensure that financial provision is made and time allowed for work to proceed without health and safety risks.

The Planning Supervisor – must undertake the following:
• Advise the client in health and safety matters.
• Develop a basic health and safety plan.
• Invoke good health and safety practices.

The Principal Contractor – must undertake the following:
• Implement the planning supervisor's health and safety plan.
• Update the plan as required.
• Co-ordinate health and safety aspects between contractors on the project.

The Designer (Architect) – must undertake the following:
• Apply design factors to reduce health and safety risk.
• Ensure designs are compatible with health and safety in the construction, maintenance and repair phases.

Health and safety matters and environmental management

For an organisation to meet the health and safety requirements of the EC Directives and their complementary national regulations, they will need to undertake a comprehensive assessment of the risks inherent in their business workplace. Depending upon the nature of the organisation this may entail little more than demonstrating common sense whilst in other organisations it may necessitate a detailed survey and review of organisational activity conducted either in-house or by external health and safety specialists. Certainly, in both cases an organisation that has anticipated a systems approach to environmental management is well placed to meet this challenge.

In the construction project situation, environmental management systems could prove to be an ideal vehicle for meeting the increasingly stringent requirements of health and safety legislation as, for example, they allow a contractor to consider systematically: the likely environmental effects of its site operation; health and safety aspects in the temporary workplace; and the effects of the project upon the surrounding inhabitants. Similarly, an environmental management system within a design practice would allow that organisation to systematically consider the implication of design factors upon health and safety during construction.

Difficulties in implementation

Perhaps the most obvious yet crucial obstacle to the wider implementation of health and safety initiatives is the financial constraint placed upon the construction industry by such stringent regulations. Whilst the larger organisations will have been complying admirably with current legislation and have little difficulty meeting EC demands, smaller organisations are not so well placed. It is such organisations who take risks in meeting health and safety requirements and tend to ignore the fact that the cost of accidents within construction can sometimes greatly exceed insured costs. Although fatal accidents in the construction process are seen to have levelled out annually at one in ten thousand employees,[12] personal risk remains much higher than other industries and therefore health and safety issues are set to retain their prominence across the EC in the years ahead.

Register of Regulations (environmental)

In addition to the three main pieces of environmental legislation (CEMAS; EA; The Framework Directive), there is a fourth group of Directives and regulations which are highly significant to the construction process. When considering an environmental management system an organisation is charged with compiling a Register of Regulations. This Register records all those EC, international and national regulations, policies and targets for meeting environmental standards within the context of the organisation's range of operations. The regulations applicable will vary from organisation to organisation within the construction industry but these regulations can generally be determined by an organisational analysis of the environmental effects of its business (see Chapter 4). Without being specific, because this would be impractical given the extent and diversity of legislation across the EC and within the various national legislation processes, the kinds of Directives and regulations that an organisation might need to take account of are, for example; emission of chlorofluorocarbons; water pollution; waste management; nuisance; noise levels; energy use, etc. It is the responsibility of the various participants to the construction process to ensure that such Directives and associated legislation are considered in the undertaking of their activities throughout the construction process.

5.5 Structure for environmental management in construction

General

This section outlines a 'basic' structure for environmental management within the construction process. Chapters 6 and 7 look in detail at the concept of environmental management in practice throughout the total construction process.

The implementation of environmental management and its systems within the construction process is fraught with difficulty. There is, as yet, no definite and recognised structure for formalised environmental management implementation within the total construction process or among all construction project types. Like so many other 'management concepts', environmental management must be somehow shoe-horned into an existing pattern of recognised procurement, design and construction management. The gradual emergence of environmental management within construction is the likely course of its development with the concept gathering support through practice, and certainly this would follow the trend led by quality management and its comparable systems approach.

Environmental management must develop within not just the traditional (consultant-led) procurement approach but within variations of non-traditional practice, each with its own set of priorities and for which environmental management must be slightly amended in focus and in approach. Whilst some aspects of environmental management are clearly defined and required to meet recognised legislation, environmental assessment and health and safety being prominent examples, other aspects follow essentially voluntary initiatives by the construction project participants. Where a client requests formal environmental management as a precondition to participate, then the demands are unequivocal, but where the initiative is left with the main contractor to function in an environmentally sound way it is more likely and understandable that other criteria will determine the project priorities leaving environmental management as a somewhat forlorn and wasted opportunity.

It is clear that environmental management is fundamentally dependent upon two stimuli: first the legislative process that invokes its principles, and second, the voluntary commitment by participants to environmentally sound construction practices. In terms of a working framework and structure within the construction process, environmental management must be heavily based on an environmentally empathic development and design phase, ably supported by a strongly sympathetic project phase, underpinned by the environmental management systems of the resource inputs.

The overall aim of environmental management in construction is to bring about long-term changes in the way the construction process gives rise to detrimental environmental effects. By placing key obligations on developers, clients, consultants, contractors and suppliers, reinforced by voluntary support, the task of ensuring environmental protection is not made any easier, but the potential for improvement is considerable and the long-term benefits achievable.

Environmental management within traditional procurement

Within the traditional (consultant-led) procurement approach, the basic structure for environmental management can be conveniently separated into three project sections:

- Project development.
- Project design.
- Project construction site.

Project development

At the project development level, environmental management is clearly an initiative of the developer, usually assisted by a specialist environmental consultant or team of consultants.

The developer is likely to support environmental management for one of three reasons:

(i) The project characteristics fall within the remit of The Environmental Assessment Directive (85/337/EEC).

(ii) The project characteristics are likely to give rise to significant environmental effects and therefore an environmental assessment is deemed necessary by the approval mechanisms.

(iii) Voluntary environmental assessment can form the basis for procedures and practices for the future operation and use of the development.

Environmental management

Any developer (or client) involved in acquiring, constructing or adapting buildings or other structures must operate within the framework of national and local regulations. Within these are the translated aspects of EC legislation and the important Environmental Assessment Directive. If the developer's proposal falls within the subject of the Directive the developer 'must' undertake an environmental assessment of the project. Otherwise, a developer need not carry out such an assessment as a mandatory requirement, although it may be requested within the approval process. Alternatively, a developer/client may see a useful need for what would be a voluntary or internal environmental assessment. A new petro-chemical plant for example would certainly in the future be subject to environmental regulations and auditing. The developer may therefore see environmental assessment as the initial basis for operation and monitoring of the plant in readiness for such auditing and control in the future.

The specialist consultant

Depending upon circumstances, the developer may or may not have appropriate in-house knowledge and expertise to conduct an environmental assessment. Where the latter is the case, the developer will appoint a specialist consultant, the environmental management consultant (see Chapter 6). At this stage the accent is upon reviewing each aspect of the proposed project in some detail to determine the likely possible environmental effects. The primary objective is, of course, to mitigate potentially major harmful environmental effects of both the construction of the development and the development in use. These basic requirements for environmental management lead to the organisational structure of the development process as shown in Figure 5.3.

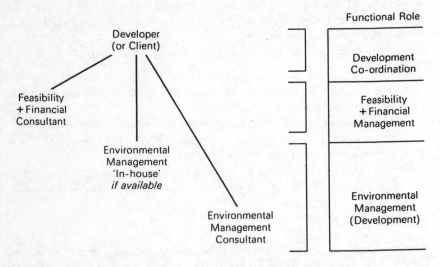

Figure 5.3   Basic structure for environmental management in the development process

The key role of the environmental management consultant or environmental management team, supported by the developer, is to:

- Conduct the environmental assessment (EA): to identify major potential environmental effects of the project.
- Prepare an environmental statement (ES): which is submitted at the developer's environmental request as part of the approval application processes.

Project design

Environmental management during the project design phase comes within the remit of the lead (design) consultant. It is the lead consultant who coordinates these specialist consultants, essential to the project, in all aspects of environmental management. The basic structure developed for this phase will serve as the basis for project construction site auditing. (See Figure 5.5.)

Health and safety

Environmental management during the project design phase is made more complex by EC Directives and translated national legislation addressing the management of health and safety in construction. Obligations are placed upon all parties, as outlined in section 5.4. It has been identified that responsibility is placed upon developers or clients to do a number of things, the most significant being to appoint a 'planning supervisor' to ensure the principles of good health and safety management are followed in the preparation of a project. In addition, designers are charged with the responsibility for ensuring that their design solutions are compatible with health and safety policies during construction. These obligations add to the basic structure for environmental management during the development phase. These additional requirements are reflected in Figure 5.4.

The key role of the planning supervisor is to:

- Advise the client in all matters of health and safety.
- Produce a basic health and safety plan.
- Ensure the principles of good health and safety management are followed in project preparation.

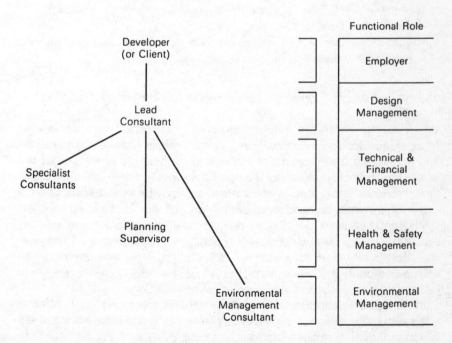

Figure 5.4   Enhanced basic structure for environmental management in the project design phase

Project construction site

At project site level, environmental management is the prerogative of the main contractor. As before, the demands of the project, its situation and circumstance, will determine the need for, and extent of, environmental management. Essentially, the main contractor should provide a framework for assessing, controlling and monitoring the impact of its activities, and the activities of others on site, upon the project's environs. Environmental management at the project site level must be developed as an extension of, and be compatible with, these principles developed during the development phase. The lead consultant will, as project overseer for the client, assume the general responsibility for this aspect although specialists may be retained from the development phase to effect this in practice given the many demands that are already assumed by the lead consultant on most construction projects.

The main contractor is likely to be driven towards environmental management for a number of reasons:

- Environmental management may be a precondition to participation demanded by the employer.
- Legislation may be applicable, for example an organisation employing over five persons must have a health and safety policy, plan and procedures of implementation.
- Voluntary implementation of environmental management may be supported for many commercial or operational reasons.

The input of 'second' organisations: sub-contractors and product suppliers

Where a main contractor implements an effective environmental management system within its organisation and successfully channels its principles and practices to the project site situation, it is obviously essential that the same standards of environmental empathy is expected of 'second' organisations; sub-contractors and suppliers. Whilst this may be desirable, the present extent of any main contractors influence over sub-contractors and suppliers will be problematic. Until there is real pressure, contractual or mandatory legislation, on goods and services to comply with environmental management facets, any main contractor will find it difficult, perhaps impossible, to source environmentally sensitive products and services. Where it is feasible to procure from such sources, this of course should be done.

In the area of health and safety management however, the main contractor is required by legislation to implement a planned programme of management which makes him responsible for the safety of all persons on site. Sub-contractors and suppliers therefore naturally fall into this category and must adhere to prevailing policy, procedures and practices.

A general structure for environmental management at project level is shown in Figure 5.5.

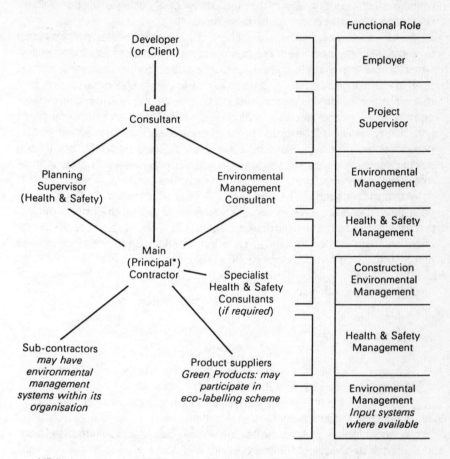

Functional Role

Developer (or Client) — Employer

Lead Consultant — Project Supervisor

Planning Supervisor (Health & Safety) — Environmental Management

Environmental Management Consultant — Health & Safety Management

Main (Principal*) Contractor — Construction Environmental Management

Specialist Health & Safety Consultants (*if required*) — Health & Safety Management

Sub-contractors *may have environmental management systems within its organisation*

Product suppliers *Green Products: may participate in eco-labelling scheme* — Environmental Management *Input systems where available*

* 'Principal' contractor (denoted in EC Directive: health & safety management)

Figure 5.5   Basic structure for environmental management during the project construction site phase

Environmental management within non-traditional procurement

As construction projects have become more technologically complex and managerially demanding and the requirements for speed of delivery, quality of service and value for money have become more finely focused, there has been considerable emphasis placed upon non-traditional forms of organisation and management to alleviate the perceived problems of traditional contracting. All of the recognised non-traditional procurement routes will create a new set of circumstances for the implementation of environmental management brought about through the re-designation of responsibilities under the different contractual arrangements.

The effects and implications of such practices cannot be determined at this time quite simply because there has been no feedback of experience upon which to base a suitable stance. Certainly, where a non-traditional form is used there should be some propensity to improve the organisation and management of environmental aspects through the shorter channels of communication and decision making between client and principal party, particularly where a true single point of control is dominant. However, it is not yet clear whether a planning supervisor, required under EC health and safety directives for example, would assume a supervisor, peer or subordinate role within a non-traditional organisation structure.

Withstanding such detail, however, it is clear that there could be tremendous advantages for environmental management within the non-traditional procurement routes, in particular those that encourage greater liaison between client and contractor, as environmental management as in concept can be introduced to the construction process at the earliest possible stage and be reflected in the thinking of clients, consultants and the contractor, through the project's documentation.

References

1   Editorial, 'Increased Road Building Threatens Wildlife Areas', *Landmarks, Landscape Design* (1993) April edition.
2   Editorial, 'Oxleas Protesters Lose High Court Battle', *Landscape Design Extra* (1993) March edition.
3   Energy Efficiency Office, 'RIBA Conference Discusses Greenhouse Effect', *Energy Management* (1990).
4   Department of Energy, *Renewable Energy in the UK: The Way Forward*, Energy Paper No. 53, HMSO (1988).
5   S. Curwell *et al.*, *Building and Health: The Rosehaugh Guide to the Design, Construction, Use and Management of Buildings*, RIBA (1990).
6   A. Leithgoe, 'Filled Up', *Landscape Design* (1993) April edition. (Leithgoe's source – DOE.)
7   Editorial, 'Eco-Audit Elicits Green Practice', *Building* (1993) 21 May edition.
8   EC, *The Environmental Assessment Directive* (1985)* (85/337/EEC) on the assessment of the effects of certain public and private projects on the environment.
9   EC, *The Environmental Assessment Directive* (1985)* (85/337/EEC) Annex III.
10   EC, *The Framework Directives* (1984) (various individual Directives).

11   Health and Safety Commission, *The Management of Health and Safety at Work Regulations*, HMSO (1992).
12   W. Leslie, 'Fresh Start for Health and Safety', *Chartered Builder* (1993) May edition.
* Denotes commonly recognised and accepted titles.

6 Environmental Assessment: Its Application to the Development Process

6.1 Introduction to environmental assessment

General

It was identified in Chapter 5 that environmental Assessment (EA), sometimes referred to as Environmental Impact Assessment (EIA), is a procedure for ensuring that the potential environmental effects of any new development or project are considered before it is allowed to proceed. There can be little doubt, if any, that all construction development has a profound effect upon its environs and a formalised procedure of environmental assessment is fundamentally crucial in seeking to mitigate potentially harmful environmental effects. Despite its current and somewhat vague status, environmental assessment is not a new concept. Its principles have been firmly applied since the early 1970s, primarily in the oil, gas and petro-chemical industries, although manufacturing and other industries have followed. Within the construction industry, its concepts became formalised in the legislative processes in the mid to late 1980s. The philosophy, concept, procedures and practices of environmental assessment have already begun to become ingrained in the construction of major developments and look set to influence a greater proportion of construction projects in the future. Its implications, therefore, are well recognised. Environmental assessment is a vital component in the concept of environmental management, with environmental management systems representing a useful tool for developers in conducting environmental assessments of their projects.

Definition

Environmental assessment was defined in Chapter 5 as:

an appraisal technique for ensuring that the potential environmental effects of any new development are identified and considered before any approval is given.

This basic definition is postulated in the absence of any one uniformly accepted definition, although a number of descriptive definitions exist. Authoritative guidance, whilst not presenting a definition *per se*, does give a clear indication of what environmental assessment is and what it seeks to achieve.

The term 'environmental assessment' describes a technique and a process by which information about the environmental effects of a project is collected, both by the developer and from other sources, and taken into account by the planning authority in forming their judgement on whether the development should go ahead.[1]

Increasing awareness of environmental assessment and its place within the concept of environmental management is leading towards broadly expanding interpretations where many believe that environmental assessment should be considered as an environmental management tool to assist planning decision makers and the development and construction process and not merely as an environmental protection measure in itself.

There is an common agreement that the fundamental aim of EIA is not to determine the balance placed by the decision-maker on environmental, compared to economic, social or other, considerations but to ensure that the decision is made on the basis of informed knowledge of the environmental consequences of that decision.[2]

Environmental assessment is, therefore, a management function aimed at providing as much information as possible to allow the most appropriate and best decision to be reached in the interests of working within the environment. Environmental assessment in practice represents a two-tier system of environmental consideration. Since environmental assessment is the prerogative of the developer it presents as environmental management 'review' (internal) mechanism which is then subject to an external evaluation (audit) by the planning authority. Environmental assessment is therefore, in practical terms, a review and audit of the development process.

EC directives on environmental assessment

It was identified in Chapter 5 that EC Directive (85/337/EEC): On the Assessment of the Effects of Certain Public and Private Projects on the Environment,[3] is a key element of EC environmental policy and was the first real act of European Legislation in environmental management. It also represented the first example of EC land use and planning legislation to be incorporated into the national physical planning procedures.

The introduction of the Directive into the national legislation processes of EC member countries has not been trouble-free. Although the Directive represents a positive and systematic approach to environmental assessment, it took almost a decade from proposal to realisation, hindered predominantly by the inherent resistance of member countries, including the UK, to change customary and recognised national planning procedures. Notwithstanding, the EC Directive was adopted by member countries in June 1985 and came into force from July 1988. It has assumed considerable prominence since.

Environmental assessment: national regulation

National procedures for environmental assessment are implemented under the EC Directive by series of regulations demanded by the approval mechanisms within each member country. The reader is therefore directed to such national legislation as applicable. Generally, procedures across member countries are similar, if not uniform, and typically follow the framework and pattern seen in the UK.

Environmental assessment: regulation in the UK

Within the UK, the requirements for environmental assessment are met through the various regulations specified in England and Wales, Scotland and Northern Ireland. The principal regulations are listed in Appendix 2. For construction projects requiring planning permission, the EC Directive is given legal effect in:

- England and Wales – by The Town and Country Planning (Assessment of Environmental Effects) Regulations, 1988.[4]
- Scotland – by The Environmental Assessment (Scotland) Regulations, 1988.[5]
- Northern Ireland – by The Planning (Assessment of Environmental Effects) Regulations (Northern Ireland), 1989.[6]

In general, the regulations applicable to England and Wales have the broadest scope of any regulations and it is therefore useful to refer to those when appreciating the requirements of the Directive. The Regulations apply to two lists, or schedules, of projects, based on Annex I and II of the EC Directive. Schedule 1 projects unreservedly require environmental assessment, whilst Schedule 2 projects may need environmental assessment if particular project oriented and environmental characteristics are significant. The criteria for determining 'significance' under national regulations are the same as those described in the EC Directive. These aspects were reviewed in Chapter 5.

Responsibility for environmental assessment

It was identified in Chapter 5 that the responsibility for initiating and conducting an environmental assessment for a project is the responsibility of the developer, usually assisted by a specialist consultant or team of consultants. The various situations in which an environmental assessment should be conducted was also identified in Chapter 5 and the reader is directed to them.

Determining the need for environmental assessment

There are essentially five situations which may lead to the undertaking of an environmental assessment. These are:

(i) *A developer applies for planning permission with no reference to environmental assessment:* because it is not necessary or the developer does not think it is necessary. In the latter case the planning authority will advise on the need.

(ii) *A developer applies for planning permission and submits an environmental statement:* because it is necessary under the EC Directive and therefore lies within national planning regulations.

(iii) *A developer applies for planning permission and asks the planning authority if an environmental assessment is necessary:* because he is unsure if the proposal falls within the scope of regulations. In this case the planning authority will advise on the need.

(iv) *The Secretary of State may independently exercise power to request environmental assessment:* where, for example, representations are made by third parties about a proposed development.

(v) *The planning authority must undertake an environmental assessment before granting itself permission for development:* because the proposal falls within national planning regulations criteria.

Participants to environmental assessment

The following list represents the principal participants to the environmental assessment process:

- The Developer – responsible for initiating and undertaking an environmental assessment of proposed development or projects.
- Specialist Consultants – appointed by the developer to conduct the environmental assessment and produce the environmental statement to support the planning application. Specialist consultants may include: landscape architect; environmental scientist; design architect; engineer; planner; other construction or life-science-related specialist.

- The Planning Authority – the public body with responsibility for considering the environmental effects of a planning application.
- The Secretary of State – involved in the environmental assessment decision-making process in specific situations.
- The Public – may become involved in environmental assessment in publically sensitive projects where, for example, they may raise issues and objections with the planning authority or to The Secretary of State.
- Statutory and other Consultees – statutory and non-statutory bodies may be asked to provide advice and information in the decision-making process. These involve such specialist organisations as The Countryside Commission; The Nature Conservancy Council; The Historic Building and Monuments Commission; etc.

The direction and focus of an environmental assessment

The primary function of environmental assessment as an environmental management tool is to systematically provide as much information as available on the environmental effects of a proposed development, such that the planning authority can base its decision to allow or not allow development with surety and futurity to the environment whilst dealing fairly with the developer and other involved parties.

The EC Directive specifies that an environmental assessment must 'identify, describe and assess' the effects of a project upon: 'human beings, fauna, flora, soil, water, air, climate and the landscape; the inter-action between the aforementioned factors; material assets and the cultural heritage'. It must therefore encompass the broad as well as the specific environmental issues.

Report: the environmental statement

Following an environmental assessment, it is the responsibility of the developer to provide the planning authority with a report – the *environmental statement* (ES). The environmental statement is:

> a publicly available document setting out the developer's own assessment of the likely environmental effects of his proposed development, which he prepares and submits in conjunction with his planning application.[7]

The environmental statement is the focus of an environmental assessment since it represents the developer's environmental management case for supporting the proposed project. The planning authority's decision to allow or refuse development may well rest on the content of this statement. Further discussion on this important aspect follows subsequently.

6.2 The process of environmental assessment within planning procedures

Aim

It was identified earlier that the developer is responsible for undertaking an environmental assessment of a proposed project and that the report, the environmental statement, is submitted as part of the planning application. There is no set form to environmental assessment or to an environmental statement but there are prescribed and detailed requirements within both the EC Directive and national regulations which must be adhered to.

The primary aim of the environmental assessment is to provide, in a systematic fashion, an objective appraisal of the significant environmental effects likely to result from the project. The environmental statement should be verifiable, that is, backed up by conclusive evidence and must include a non-technical summary, or what is essentially a lay-person's guide because the report may be read by non-technical persons and members of the general public.

Developer's consultation with interested parties

At the start of this chapter the importance of recognising environmental assessment as a management tool to aid decision making and not as an environmental protection measure *per se* was postulated. Early consultation between the developer and organisations, institutions or bodies with an interest in the environmental effects of the proposed development is essential. Dialogue must be established at the start of the planning process if difficulties, problems and ambiguities are to be avoided. Environmental assessment, both as a statutory requirement and management concept, should therefore become almost a state of mind from the developer's notional idea of development. It should certainly be an intrinsic aspect of the developer's site selection. In this way, the environmental effects on a specific site can be extensively reviewed before commitment is given to it and where major problems are identified alternative sites may be considered for better suitability.

Within the regulatory processes, although a developer may not be bound to consult the planning authority prior to submitting a planning application, it is sensible to do so – first, because consultation develops the useful working dialogue alluded to previously, and second, because the planning authority may be able to provide useful information on the project's environs. More pertinent perhaps, the planning authority will be able to air their likely concerns for the proposal, interpret public feeling, and identify potential issues which may have gone unnoticed to the developer.

As some development projects are highly sensitive, due to their nature, scope or size, a developer may wish to consult the planning authority in confidence in the initial stages, although should the developer seek formal ruling on, for example, the need to undertake an environmental assessment of his proposal, the planning authority is bound to make the information public.

The environmental statement: its content and description

In England and Wales, the formal requirements for content of an environmental statement is set out in the Town and Country Planning (Assessment of Environmental Effects) Regulations (1988)[4] and in Scotland and Northern Ireland within their Regulations[5,6] respectively. These Regulations were identified earlier in this chapter. In addition, authoritative guidance is available in a number of Department of Environment (DoE) publications.[7,1]

The reader is directed to the aforementioned authoritative sources, in particular the latter,[1] as it presents a comprehensive checklist of aspects the developer should consider for inclusion in an environmental statement. Although not intended as a prescribed structure, the checklist does form an excellent outline framework for the preparation of an environmental statement.

Whilst several informed sources suggest an appropriate framework for environmental statements, within the scope of national regulations there are typically five main sections within which detailed information must be provided. These are:

(i)   Information describing the project.
(ii) Information describing the project site and its environs.
(iii) Information describing the assessment of environmental effects.
(iv) Information describing the measures to be taken in mitigating the effects.
(v)   Information describing the risks of accidents and hazardous development.*

* Information in this category is not specifically covered by the EC Directive, nor in national regulations, but may be encompassed by other statutory legislation. In the construction industry for example, it is inevitable that The Management of Health and Safety at Work Regulations (1992)[8] will have significant influence over the project's activities. Information concerning the potential risk of accidents or hazardous installation should therefore feature within the content of an environmental statement.

An environmental statement may not need to cover each and every aspect of a project's potential environmental effects. After all, each project will have different characteristics and different requirements. The environmental statement must, however, cover the project's significant environmental effects. Some aspects will therefore be covered in considerable detail whilst others will be afforded brief attention.

The early consultation and continuing dialogue between the developer and the planning authority, previously referred to, is essential to ensuring that the developer's submission meets with the satisfaction of the planning authority. The information that constitutes the content and description of the environmental statement is left to the discretion of the developer although integration rather than isolation may mean the difference between providing the planning authority with the right information and the wrong information. Once the environmental statement is submitted it becomes a formal part of the planning application and the planning authority has the right to demand additional information if it feels that the content and description is deficient in any way.

Statutory, non-statutory and other consultees

Environmental legislation dictates that public bodies with statutory environmental responsibilities must be consulted by the planning authority when a planning application is considered. The various Regulations[4,5,6] and other guideline publications[1] provide a list of such 'statutory consultees'. Where statutory consultees are to become involved in the process of environmental assessment, they will be notified along with the developer by the planning authority. Statutory consultees are required to provide the developer with any information pertinent to the environmental assessment. It is the developer's responsibility to contact the statutory consultees and information is provided strictly upon request. The statutory consultees provide information solely in their possession and does so in an objective and unbiased way. Any formal opinions and advice from the statutory consultees is considered at a later stage in the decision-making process.

In addition to contacting statutory consultees, the developer may wish to seek information and the expertise of other bodies during the course of the environmental assessment. These 'non-statutory consultees' may have knowledge particular to the project site, its environs or its potential environmental effects. Other consultees may be local residents, businesses or organisations with an interest in the proposed development. Whilst the developer is under no obligation to advise or consult such groups, it was identified earlier that wider dialogue can be useful in identifying and understanding likely environmental effects, in addition to public feelings and concerns.

Conducting an environmental assessment

The methodological approach adopted and practices used to conduct an effective environmental assessment leading to a satisfactory environmental statement will depend upon the individual characteristics of the proposed project, its site and the information available on which to base the assessment. Each development proposed is different, perhaps unique, and for this reason, if no other, the presentation of a definitive guideline is precluded. There are, however, techniques used for environmental assessment that determine a common theme and support the use of common elements of study and instruments of assessment. Such methodological approach follows in this chapter.

The principal mechanism of data collection for environmental assessment is the environmental site survey (ESS). This enables the environmental consultant, working on behalf of the developer, to make a first-hand assessment of the project's potential for environmental impact and effects. The concepts and procedures involved in environmental site surveys are not discussed in this section specifically. They are, however, explained in Chapter 7 where the lead consultant's site survey at the design stage and the contractor's site survey at the construction stage are discussed.

Submitting the environmental statement

The environmental statement is submitted as part of the planning application to the planning authority. The planning authority will judge if the environmental statement has provided them with the necessary information on which to base their considerations. Where an application is submitted in brief outline form, the planning authority must still have sufficient information on the likely environmental effects of the proposal to enable them to reach a decision. It cannot pass on an application with insufficient environmental information as this would completely undermine the subsequent control processes.

The developer must, upon submitting a planning application, publish a public notice of intent to develop and state where and when the environmental statement may be inspected. This is usually placed in a local newspaper or similar community publication. The developer should ensure that sufficient copies of the environmental statement are available for interested members of the public and, in addition, provide a copy, either directly or through the planning authority, to each of the statutory consultees.

Action by the planning authority

Upon receipt of the planning application and the environmental statement, the planning authority will record the submission on the Planning Register. In terms of the formal time-frame for processing an application, the calendar is seen to commence upon receipt. Statutory consultees have a minimum of fourteen days to comment and a sixteen-week basic period for determination of the application commences.

The planning authority will send a copy of the planning application together with the environmental statement to the office of the Secretary of

State. This is essential to the monitoring process, in particular on those projects which are likely to be referred for decision to higher jurisdiction.

Collecting further information

It has already been mentioned that if the planning authority sees fit it can request the developer to furnish additional information to supplement the submitted environmental statement. This is likely where insufficient information has been provided, where additional information can clarify the position of likely environmental effects, or where further information is needed to verify reports made. Such a situation is only likely to result where there has been little dialogue between the developer and the planning authority. Usually close liaison ensures that difficulty does not occur. Statutory, non-statutory and other consultees may however raise issues which requires the provision of supplementary information.

Specialist guidance

The planning authority may, at their own discretion, refer the environmental statement to specialist consultants who can advise them for example on those specific environmental aspects that may lie outside their own range of knowledge or expertise.

Determination of the planning application

Within current procedure, the planning authority should determine the outcome of a planning application within sixteen weeks from the date of submission (or sixteen weeks from the receipt of the environmental statement where this was submitted after the planning application), although this may be extended with the developer's agreement.

Like all planning applications, the planning authority may refuse permission or grant permission, conditionally or unconditionally. Should the planning authority need a broader environmental statement it can request the developer to provide supplementary information to facilitate its decision. In the event that the planning authority fails to reach a decision within the sixteen-week period the developer can refer the matter to the Secretary of State.

The right of appeal

The developer has, given certain outcomes (adverse decision, or failure to determine within the time-frame), a right of appeal to the Secretary of State. The office of the Secretary of State will appoint inspectors to examine the planning application and the environmental statement and collect any information they deem to be appropriate in advising on a ruling.

The routes to environmental assessment

Figures 6.1, 6.2 and 6.3 illustrate the various routes to environmental assessment which are described within this section.

6.3 The principal role of the environmental consultant

General

While some larger developers and client organisations may have sufficient in-house knowledge and expertise to conduct their own environmental assessments, the vast majority will not. Most will rely upon the appointment of a specialist, the *environmental consultant*. In recent years, environmental consultants have emerged from a variety of backgrounds, some being more suited to the demands of environmental management than others. As environmental management becomes more greatly accepted within the construction industry and environmental assessment becomes more entrenched within the regulatory processes, the need for highly specialist, not merely adept, multi-disciplinary teams is becoming overwhelmingly evident.

Growth in the environmental consultancy sector

Over the last twenty years, and in particular the last five years, the growth in the number of environmental consultancies has risen dramatically, in fact fourfold between 1985 and 1993. As experience with environmental management grows, quite naturally developers, clients and consultants are seeking better and informed ways to conduct environmental assessment. Whereas in recent years, organisations involved in environmental assessment were seen to come from a single discipline, now a multi-skilled approach is coming to the fore. Given the sometimes wide ranging, yet specialist nature of environmental assessment, a developer's needs may only be met by such a broadly based team. Some multi-disciplinary consultancies operate as environmental project managers that advise their client from the development phase through to construction on site. This rapid development and focus in environmental consultancy has lead to considerable concern that environmental assessment is perhaps developing into a vehicle to be ridden by those whose environmental intentions are less well placed. Despite such criticism however, there is little doubt that environmental management is operating within a market that is currently in a state of flux and that until the environmental consultancy sector settles down and consolidates there will be some variability in the quality of the environmental assessment process.

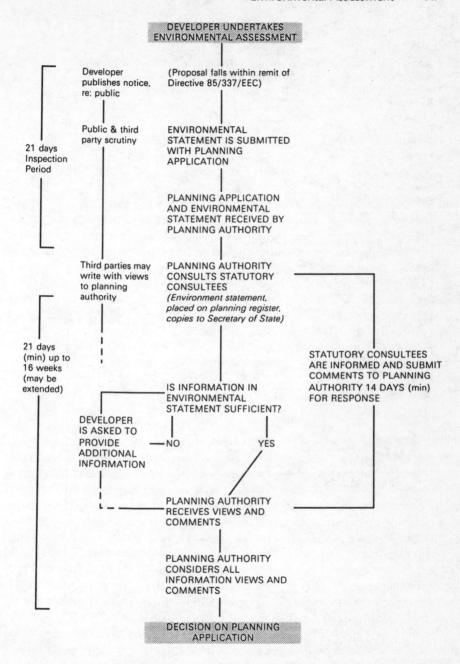

Figure 6.1 Submission of environmental statement in conjunction with planning application, where the proposal clearly falls within the remit of the environmental assessment directive

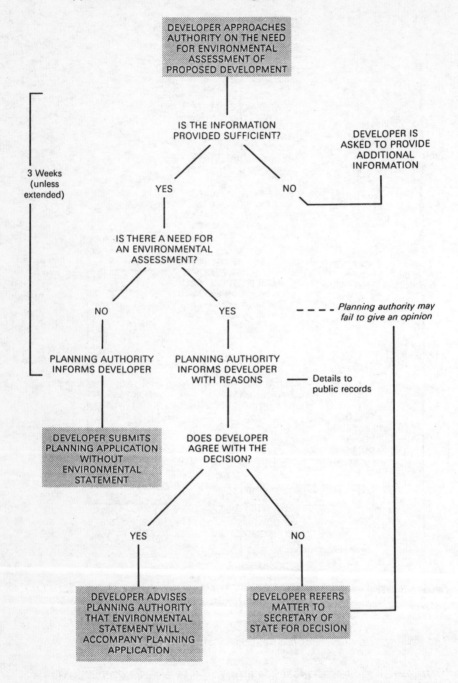

Figure 6.2　The route for determining the need for an environmental statement where the developer requests guidance from the planning authority

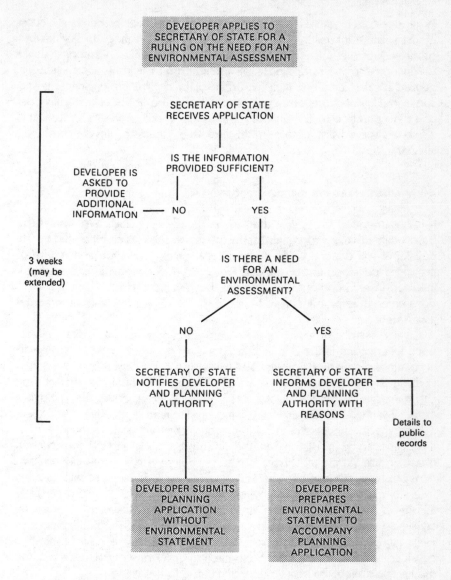

Figure 6.3   *The route for determining the need for an environmental statement where the developer requests guidance from the Secretary of State*

The skill profile of environmental consultants

Evidence suggests that a considerable proportion of environmental assessments are conducted by consultants from a science or engineering background. This is hardly surprising if one considers the likely orientation of the larger developers and client organisations operating within the construction industry. More interesting perhaps is the considerable range of skills across other environmental consultancy practices which take in amongst other disciplines: architecture; landscape architecture; environmental sciences; geotechnical science; geography; urban planning; mining engineering and surveying; horticulture; and agriculture. Clearly, the ability of any individual or single practice to match the all-embracing skill profile is limited and reinforces the advantage of a multi-disciplinary team to provide combined specialist input.

Environmental project management

It is not intended to suggest that any particular consultant type forms the base for effective environmental assessment. The consultant appointed by the developer will depend upon many criteria, chiefly the type and nature of proposed development or project. From the major professions extensively involved in environmental assessment, however, the landscape consultant does emerge as prominent and central to the objectives of environmental assessment.

Given the inherent nature of the construction process and its direct effects upon its environs, landscape architecture is an essential aspect of any environmentally sympathetic project. The landscape consultant is able to address perhaps the most damaging aspect of construction, visual disturbance, and can reinforce this with specialist knowledge of, for example, the ecological aspect. Moreover, landscape consultants tend to feature greatly in the project management aspects of development where environmental management as a concept can be translated from the development phase to the construction phase on site. Whilst, for the reasons stated before, the landscape consultant does not have, nor can be expected to have, the wide range of skills needed to encompass all aspects of environmental assessment, they can certainly assume a useful role in aiding the environmental assessment process by acting as one of the developer's main environmental project advisors or even being project co-ordinator. Many large clients are now tending to consider a project management approach to environmental assessment and this certainly seems to be its orientation in the future.

The role of the environmental consultant

The principal role of the environmental consultant within the environmental assessment process is to undertake the following:

- Liaise with the developer (his client) on all aspects of environmental assessment.

- Appraise the developer on matters of environmental legislation and regulations.
- Liaise with other specialist consultants, where required.
- Liaise with the planning authority (where requested by the client) upon matters concerning the environmental statement.
- Liaise with statutory, non-statutory and other consultees who become involved in environmental assessment.
- Undertake an environmental site survey (ESS) to collect, collate and analyse the information necessary for the environmental assessment of the proposal.
- Provide the environmental statement, submitted with the developer's planning application to the planning authority.

In addition, the environmental consultant may be asked by the developer to:

- Act in the capacity of environmental consultant during the briefing, design and procurement phases.
- Act as environmental consultant during the construction phase on-site.

6.4 Conducting an environmental assessment and preparing the environmental statement

General

It was identified earlier in this chapter that the individual, perhaps even unique, characteristics of each development project inherently precludes the presentation of a standard definitive guideline for undertaking an environmental assessment. The environmental statement, resulting from an environmental assessment, must reflect the particular characteristics of the project, its site, and its environs. It was also recognised that there is a common thread running through national, European and international conceptualisations of environmental assessment such that common elements of study and instruments of assessment are realised. These form the base for a sound methodological approach to conducting an environmental assessment and preparing the environmental statement for any proposed project.

The stages of environmental assessment

There are seven principal elements in the process of environmental assessment. These are supported by one further element, essential to the realisation of success but which is frequently understated. These elements are:

(i)   Project description.
(ii) Screening.

(iii) Scoping.
(iv) Baseline studies.
(v) Impact prediction.
(vi) Mitigation assessment.
(vii) Environmental statement.
(viii) Environmental monitoring.

Project description

This is:

> a sufficient and clear description of the project together with details of its location.

Although detailed information *per se* is not required at this initial stage, the developer must provide the planning authority with sufficient information to judge whether an environmental assessment is necessary. The temptation to perhaps limit the information provided such that the planning authority might be misled into determining an environmental assessment as unnecessary should be resisted: first, because the planning authority treats this stage in the planning process most seriously as it lays the basis for the whole process; and second, because the dialogue for determination of a planning application (see section 6.2) is fostered upon open and helpful communication. It is in the developer's best interests to furnish as much information as necessary to the planning authority and to act in a wholly co-operative manner.

Screening

Screening is

> the process of determining, for a particular project, the need for an environmental assessment.

Within the UK regulatory process the planning authority assumes responsibility for screening all proposed developments, whether they come under Schedule 1, those projects for which environmental assessment is compulsory, or Schedule 2, those projects which may have significant environmental effects and warrant assessment. There is, however, considerable variation in procedural readiness across the UK, despite the legislative rigour that prevails. Some planning authorities have very limited experience of managing the environmental assessment process while others have detailed procedures and guidelines. Whilst determining the need for environmental assessment of Schedule 1 projects is clearly unambiguous to all planning authorities, there may be considerable variability in policy for determining Schedule 2 projects across planning authorities. Unfortunately, the practical procedures of the screening process can be somewhat imprecise and is frequently open to interpretation.

Scoping

Scoping is concerned with:

directing the environmental assessment towards aspects of specific importance.

Scoping is a vital step in the environmental assessment process as it must clearly identify those aspects which require detailed study and analysis and forms the basis for impact prediction of environmental effects. The result of scoping is the development of an environmental assessment programme or schedule which relates particular attributes of the development process to environmental aspect. Such a programme provides direction to the subsequent baseline studies. In practice, scoping often focuses upon the requirements of Schedule 3 of the environmental regulations as these specify the requirements for the environmental statement. Whilst this is useful as a basic outline it is rather insufficient for the detailed characteristics of an effective environmental assessment.

Baseline studies

Baseline studies are concerned with:

the identification of the significant environmental impacts that must be assessed.

Baseline studies follow on naturally from, or even form an inherent part of, scoping. The environmental assessment programme or schedule developed during scoping will direct the baseline study. This will provide information on:

- The detailed description of the project.
- The project's environs.
- The social dimension.

Impact prediction

This is concerned with:

assessing the potential for environmental effect of those aspects identified during scoping and baseline studies.

The focus of this aspect is, by definition, on determining the likely effect of specific project aspects upon the environment. Naturally it is difficult, frequently impossible, to predict potential environmental effects with any degree of accuracy. Usually, environmental impact prediction is a subjective description of what will happen, known from experience, or what might happen based upon reasoning or expectation. Strictly, analysis should lead to accurate prediction based on verifiable information. It should be determined and not based on judgement or guesswork. In practice, environmental assessment should involve detailed investigation by experienced consultants and the resulting information presented in clear and unambiguous form, based on sound common sense reasoning of accurate data.

Mitigation assessment

This focuses upon:

> *consideration of the measures to be taken to alleviate or minimise environmental effects.*

The accent of this section is towards summarising recommendations, developed during the analytical and predictive processes, aimed at mitigating the environmental effects of the project. It is appropriate for the measures of mitigation to incorporate aspects of project site layout and construction, in addition to the design solution, as this will act as a useful management tool throughout the total construction process. It is essential that the developer provides detailed information on this aspect with the utmost care and are ready to request further information if they feel that mitigation measures have not been fully thought-through or explained adequately.

The environmental statement

An authoritative definition[7] of the term 'environmental statement' was presented earlier in this chapter. In practice, the statement is the mechanism by which the developer places the findings of the environmental assessment before the planning authority. The extent and detail of an environmental statement will be determined by the characteristics and situation of the particular project. Whilst some statements are a brief, almost superficial, overview of a project, others are perhaps over-detailed. The environmental statement should always be commensurate with need which is essentially based on the salient and major project aspects likely to give rise to potentially harmful environmental effects.

An accompaniment to for the environmental statement is the *Non-technical Summary*. This should be produced as a separate document to the main environmental statement. Its purpose is to provide a lay-person's guide to the project and should be written in simple, non-technical and jargon-free text and be simply formated to assist ease of understanding. The non-technical summary should enable a wider audience, i.e. the public, to acquaint themselves with the findings of the environmental assessment such that they can make comments, if desired, to the planning authority or other arbiter of the planning proposal.

Presentation and form of the environmental statement

In addition to the authoritative sources mentioned earlier in this chapter,[7.1] the reader is directed to Appendix 3 of this work. This presents a typical environmental statement which illustrates some of the elements of environmental assessment explained in this chapter. It is emphasised that although the statement represents a genuine submission, the names, places, details and any other distinguishing characteristics have been changed and it is merely a guide to the types of environmental statements that are being submitted.

Environmental monitoring

Environmental monitoring is concerned with:

> *monitoring the environmental effects of the project, if and when the project is given approval to proceed.*

Environmental monitoring is an understated yet essential aspect of the environmental assessment process. It has not yet become customary to include this element in the formal programme of environmental assessment. This is to be expected, however, given that it is not a developmental element but one which only becomes recognised once the project progresses beyond the planning approval process. Environmental monitoring is essential as a concept, as it provides the sound base upon which wider principles and practices will undoubtedly advance in the future. It is, in addition, rapidly becoming a prerequisite to the wider issues of environmental regulation and auditing schemes and looks set to play an even more significant role in the future.

Environmental assessment: the contribution of environmental management systems

Whilst many construction projects do not fall within the legislative criteria for environmental assessment, there is a growing trend among developers and clients to undertake environmental assessments on a voluntary basis. Many organisations see this as a positive projection of their commitment to and actions towards environmental protection. Such developers commission environmental assessment to inform the briefing, design and construction processes and to ensure that the resulting development represents the best environmental option that is practically achievable. Many organisations will find that such an approach fits in well with its current organisational commitment to the environment, which is likely to be displayed through its environmental management system.

An organisation that operates an environmental management system will be in an ideal position to undertake environmental assessments of its development projects, as it will, through application and experience, have already identified the environmental effects of its business and needs only to focus upon the environmental effects of the project site. Organisations who are, and are seen to be, environmentally empathic will find they can respond much better to the requirements of the planning process than those who are not. They are also seen by the regulatory processes and the outside world as organisations who have due regard and respect for the environment. Environmental management systems give the organisation the framework, structure and rigour to undertake environmental assessment effectively which helps the process itself, but moreover, it allows the organisation to better see the project in relation to the organisation's wider activities.

Many organisations also find that environmental management systems are essential to environmental monitoring. Environmental monitoring can benefit a developer in a number of ways. First, any deviation from the predicted environmental impact assessment can be seen at an early stage and therefore management can respond quickly and more effectively. In this way, monitoring is developed into an auditing and review mechanism, which is the likely long-term development of the environmental assessment process. Second, environmental monitoring is a useful source of information to the developer. It may be used to defend claims for environmental damage, used for verification purposes in regulatory inspections, and used to support the organisation's activities in certification schemes. Third, environmental monitoring allows the organisation to see the longer-term environmental picture, and information generated from one environmental assessment and monitoring initiative can be used purposefully on the next project and so on, leading to an environmental database with the organisation.

Those larger organisations who have an environmental management system in place are undoubtedly likely to use it as a basis for procuring their projects. It can give them the necessary management rigour to better control the development, briefing, design and construction processes and be easily extended to form the basis of operating procedures and working practices within the use of the finished development.

An environmental management system can benefit the developer when conducting an environmental assessment in the following ways:

- By producing the necessary outline, framework and structure within the organisation to get the best from environmental assessment.
- In-house expertise, where available, may assist the appointed team of environmental consultants.
- The environmental effects of the developer's activities will already have been identified.
- Information on the developer's past and current environmental performance will be known.
- There is a lesser focus on the developer and more attention given to the project site and its environs.
- Information is gathered over the longer-term through environmental monitoring which provides a wider range of knowledge than might otherwise be available and information which should be more reliable.

Environmental assessment case study: shoreline petrochemical handling and distribution facility

An environmental assessment was conducted on a proposed petrochemical handling and distribution facility located on a major river estuary. Although the situation of the plant would be well sheltered within the existing topography and natural features of the area and was to be positioned alongside neighbouring petrochemical facilities, concern was raised as to the possible effects on the shoreline and to its aesthetic aspect when viewed from particular vantage points.

Environmental assessment considered both the neighbouring and long-distance views from both land and sea. This was aided considerably with both aerial photographs and panoramic photomontages upon which the proposed development could be overlaid to give an impression of the aesthetic implications. In addition, a detailed environmental effects evaluation was carried out on both the adjacent landscape and marine environment to assess potential hazards to the local environs.

Particular mitigation measures were identified as essential to the scheme, for example, the re-routing of the pipeline from its originally intended course and a shelter bed of trees and shrubs in one particular area to reduce aesthetic disturbance to nearby properties. The project was granted planning permission in due course.

Environmental assessment case study: shopping complex

A major environmental assessment was conducted on a area designated for the development of a new shopping complex. The location was particularly sensitive as it involved an area of recognised natural interest. Due to the diverse and extensive infrastructure needed to support the shopping centre, a multi-disciplinary team of consultants was employed to consider the aspects of landscape, ecology, traffic and, of course, human and commercial interference upon the area.

Having considered the likely effects upon the proposed site and the over-whelming mitigation measures that would be demanded, it was judged that an alternative site be located and therefore planning permission was refused.

Environmental assessment case study: industrial brine reservoir

An environmental assessment was carried out to evaluate a proposal for a new brine reservoir associated within an existing industrial complex but situated close to a new residential area. Assessment considered the intrusion of the reservoir upon the visual and topographical situation. Interest focused mainly upon the profile and height of the proposed retaining embankments and the screening demanded from the neighbouring residential area. Mitiga-tion measures determined the need for additional screening in the form of additional embankments, trees and shrubs, but also identified the need for safety and security measures should a member of the public, a child for example, venture onto the site. Particular attention was therefore paid to providing unobtrusive but effective security fencing. In addition, attention was drawn specifically to the efficacy of the brine retention medium to be used in the construction of the embankments to ensure that potential leakage was unlikely. Planning permission was granted for this project subject to implementing the additional mitigation measures.

6.5 Environmental assessment: experience of procedures and practices

Evaluation on the effectiveness of environmental assessment

As use of environmental assessment procedures increase and experience grows, greater attention is being directed towards the determination of its effectiveness and worth to the planning process. In 1989, the Environmental Impact Assessment (EIA) Centre was the first to identify the main problems associated with environmental assessment since its formal introduction in the mid to late 1980s. It highlighted that environmental assessments were of variable and dubious quality, that there was a general unfamiliarity with the procedures and practices involved and that local authorities allowed many projects to elude the assessment process. Clearly there was cause for con-cern. Following these observations, the Institute of Environmental Assessment (IEA) was established, its mission *to improve the quality of environmental impact assessments*. Both the IEA and the EIA Centre serve as guardians to monitor the practical implementation of environmental assessment within the UK.

Following their air of concern, the EIA Centre produced the first official review of the environmental assessment process.[9] This reinforced their earlier comments and presented sound recommendations for much needed improvements. Similarly, a report by the IEA[10] reviewed practical experience with environmental assessment identifying further issues and problems. Later research[11, 12] marks out a similar path, leading to the identification of some serious issues and matters to be addressed within the environmental assessment process if success in the future is to be secured.

A review of some of the issues and problems

The environmental statement itself is probably the most significant element in any environmental assessment as it reflects those key and vital issues of the project and presents the basis for liaison, consultation and decision-making. It is only to be expected, therefore, that much study and research focuses upon the environmental statement as a reflection of the effectiveness and worth of the environmental assessment process. The main issues and problems are presented and whilst it is somewhat certain that the list will not be exhaustive, it does give a clear indication of the type and magnitude of concern that currently prevails.

Enforcement of environmental assessment regulations

At this time it is more than likely that many local authority planning departments, responsible for enforcing environmental assessment regulations, will have little or no experience in the appropriate procedures and practices. Investigations[13] reveal that well over a half of such local authorities had not handled a planning application with an environmental statement. In addition, it appears that some projects which qualify for environmental assessment are not complying with the regulations. The principal reason for the inconsistent enforcement of environmental assessment regulations is seen to be unfamiliarity with the regulations and a general lack of knowledge in the procedures and practices.

Time-frame for the decision-making process

Within the regulations which govern planning applications, the local authority has sixteen weeks from the date of receipt of the environmental statement to determine the application and respond. There is, of course, some leeway by mutual agreement as identified in an earlier chapter. Studies[9] show that, in general, only one-half of planning applications with environmental statements were determined within the designated time frame. In another investigation,[10] an average time to determine a planning application with environmental statement was thirty-six weeks. Clearly, the time-frame for determining projects is grossly inadequate at this time as current legislative time-frames appear somewhat meaningless in practice.

The quality of environmental statements

Research[10] shows that where environmental assessments have been evaluated for quality, almost two-thirds have been judged to be unsatisfactory. Other studies[2] indicate some improvement over time as one would expect, yet there remains a considerable inadequacy in the performance of environmental assessments undertaken, reflected in the poor general quality of environmental statements submitted. Although there is likely to be some variation in thoroughness of environmental assessments undertaken, due to project specific characteristics it is identified that relatively small projects with shorter environmental statements are those which demonstrate a lower standard of quality. It is undoubtedly that the degree of experience of the developer is significant, with smaller organisations having little or no experience whilst the larger developer and client organisations have a better range of knowledge and experience reflecting in their more accomplished environmental assessment procedures.

Presentation of the environmental statement

A number of studies[11,12] draws attention to the often parlous quality of presentation of findings from environmental assessments. Environmental statements are frequently criticised for their lack of objectivity, over-description and most importantly the use of qualititative and statistical data without detailed analysis and verifiable conclusions. Many environmental statements appear to be deliberately qualitative and descriptive in nature without being backed up by sound quantitative material. This is not surprising, however, as requirements call for a detailed statement supplemented by a non-technical summary and it is likely that many developers are torn between the extremes of complexity and simplicity, in practice fulfilling neither requirement adequately.

The true cost of environmental assessment

Whilst it is generally difficult to obtain information in respect of cost implications of environmental assessment, research[9] does suggest conflicting estimations as to incurred costs. While a large proportion suggest that environmental assessment causes a slight increase in the developer's costs, a small but significant proportion hold that environmental assessment leads to a much greater increase in development costs. It would not be unreasonable to suggest that an increase in development costs of something between 1 and

5 per cent might be expected depending upon the project circumstances at the time.

Contribution to environmental protection

Whilst the importance of environmental assessment to the concept of environmental management cannot be overstated, its contribution as an environmental protection measure has been brought into question. A number of studies[9,11] reinforce the effectiveness and worth of the general concepts, with one study indicating that in two-thirds of projects examined, modification to the proposals were made during the planning process. Although developers and consultants suggested that these modifications would have been made anyway in the course of planning discussion, the findings nevertheless suggest that the environmental assessment process does make a tangible contribution to the decision-making processes and, in so doing, contributes to environmental protection. However, the fact that it is well known that there is some infringement of the UK regulations and documented complaints received by the European Commission under Directive 85/337/EEC shows that there is some discontent and contradictory evidence to the support of environmental assessment as an environmental protection mechanism.

Research in the course of writing, substantiated by several of the referenced sources, identifies the problem of some developers lacking initiative and procedures to undertake an effective environmental assessment. In contrast to those developers who had little knowledge and experience, there was a small group of larger developers/clients who through their commitment to internal environmental management systems found themselves in the advantageous position of readily understanding current environmental regulations and knowing their way through the practical maze of environmental assessment. Clearly those organisations who already have a systems approach to environmental management are in a much better position to respond to the demands of the environmental planning processes.

Advocacy documentation

Further and ostensibly qualitative study,[11] eliciting the views of practitioners in local authorities, raises attention to the use of the environmental statement as an advocacy document aimed solely at easing the route through the planning processes. It is identified that even where local authorities work closely with developers to determine the direction and focus of an assessment, local authorities really have little control over the quality of the environmental statement since developers may cover all the significant environmental impacts identified in scoping but only cover the aspects superficially in practice.

Specialist advice

The same study identified that where environmental statements were found to be ambiguous in content or quality, the local authority went to considerable expense of employing teams of specialist consultants to review the statement and advise the developer of apparent deficiency. It was highlighted that the view is held amongst some local authorities that such difficulties are almost designed into the process in its current position. In examining the time-frame for determination of a planning application it was seen that developers sometimes took months to prepare the environmental statement but the planning authority had no control over this. Exceeding the stipulated sixteen-week determination period appears to occur quite readily, and whilst local authorities appear to readily accept this as the norm it is not surprising if they are in fact employing large teams of environmental specialists to evaluate the submission as the current system does not take such a course of action into full account.

Additional concerns

Research in the course of compiling this book, supported by the empirical evidence of several studies, [9,10,11,12] has led to a number of concerns, issues and problems, other than those already raised. These can be summarised as follows:

- There is undoubtedly a general lack of understanding of the requirements for environmental assessment amongst developers and local authorities, and also an absence of detailed knowledge of the procedures and processes involved.
- Wholly systematic procedures are not being utilised by developers in current environmental assessments.
- Frequently, environmental assessment is being used merely in an attempt to manipulate and sway an ambiguous planning application.
- Few environmental statements appear to present innovative aspects but rather present existing data and little or no original thought as to environmental opportunities.
- There tends to be a lack of objectivity in the presentation of the findings where objectivity would lead to better options being identified.
- In many environmental statements there is little or no justification for statements made and ideas are not, in the main, well supported by evidence or reason.
- Where projects identify multiple environmental effects, rather than review them in combination to assess their combined and real effects, they are dealt with individually and somewhat superficially which deflects their true level of significance.

- There appears to be weak attention given to perhaps the most significant aspect of environmental assessment, that of measures considered to mitigate environmental effects.
- Environmental assessments, in the main, tend to focus upon the site itself and pay little attention to the potential design implications or environmental effects of the construction process.
- In environmental statement presentation, there is little or no thought demonstrated to interrelating the main phases of the construction process; development; design; construction; and use.
- As the accent of an environmental statement is to provide a clear and succinct view of the project, important issues can be hidden and go unnoticed by all but the most vigilant regulatory process.
- Summaries of environmental statements tend to be weak and fail to identify with clarity the main thrust of the argument.
- Environmental statements are often submitted without the required non-technical summary. The summary, designed to inform the lay-person, is given little attention by many developers.

Concern within the European Commission

The European Commission is constantly vigilant of the potential infringement of its environmental assessment Directive, 85/337/EEC, in member countries. In 1991, having received complaints relating to the implementation of the Directive within the UK, the Commission made specific reference to projects where the Commission considered that their had been a breach in the requirements of the Directive. Due to the ongoing position of these projects and their high level of political and public sensitivity they are not reviewed here but are considered in one of the empirical research sources to the work.[11] The issue directly raised by the intervention of the European Commission in some quarters is whether the Commission is on the side of environmental protection, as indeed it should be, or whether it bows to the political pressure from its member states and falls on the side of development. Certainly it appears that whilst it supports the framework and structure for environmental management systems and environmental assessment across member countries, there appear to be some ambiguities and loopholes in the policing of the process at national level, which allows infringement to take place, and perhaps while the Commission is in a position to remedy the situation it is not perhaps sufficiently forceful with its improvement proposals.

Proposals for improvement

Those difficulties and problems experienced within the UK with the environmental assessment process and which were perhaps originally perceived as early teething problems are still apparent to a large extent today. The concern and issues raised through many investigations and by many parties demonstrate a high degree of commonality and a strong trend that all is not perhaps as well as it might be. There appear to be several fundamental issues and many specific issues that need to be addressed if environmental assessment as a concept is to be consolidated as a wholly reliable mechanism for appraising and auditing the development process.

European Commission Proposals

Following an extensive review of the implementation of the EC environmental assessment Directive, the Commission has proposed a number of significant changes to its constitution that seek to eliminate some of the Directive's apparent ambiguity. At the time of writing these proposals are:

- To introduce a new directive on Strategic Environmental Assessment.
- To reinforce the significance of Annex I projects (those which are subject to mandatory environmental assessment) by grouping Annex II projects within Annex I.
- To make the requirements of Annex III (information to be included in an environmental statement) compulsory.
- To make 'scoping' (directing the environmental assessment process towards aspects of specific importance) a formal requirement.
- To make the selection of 'alternatives' standard practice, including a 'non-action' alternative.

The implementation of the European Commission proposals should help to ensure that the significant environmental impacts of projects are considered more thoughtfully and comprehensively and should, on balance, generally improve the quality of environmental assessment and environmental statements in the future.

Department of Environment proposals

In the Department of Environment (DOE) Report,[9] a considerable number of recommendations were postulated, the significant facet being that no alterations were needed to the basic framework of the environmental assessment procedures. These recommendations address some of the problems identified, the most significant being:

- There should be more guidance on the methodology for undertaking environmental assessment.
- There should be more guidance on the interpretation of 'significant environmental effects'.
- There should be better review criteria to assist planning authorities with their evaluation of environmental statements.

- There should be provision to formally extend the sixteen week determination period where appropriate.

Proposals by The Council for the Protection of Rural England

In 1992, The Council for the Protection of Rural England (CPRE) published a report[14] which proposed significant amendments to the EC Directive. These are as follows:

- That each member state establishes an Environmental Assessment Authority who would assume responsibility for ensuring that the requirements of the Directive were implemented.
- That the developer must publish a 'scoping' document on which relevant and interested parties could openly comment.
- That the responsible local authority must publish their opinion on the adequacy of the developer's submission, in particular aspects relating to: compliance with the directive; the likely environmental impacts of the development; and the mitigation of environmental effects considered.
- That a decision on the proposal would not be made until the Environmental Assessment Authority considered the submission to be acceptable.

These proposals would perhaps bring into line the UK's environmental assessment procedures with those of other countries worldwide. Certainly the independent audit of the development process is welcomed by some groups although there remains some ambiguity over who would be responsible for specific aspects of the review processes, the planning authority or the independent body.

The move towards an independent review body

In the UK, the developer is responsible for identifying the scope and content of an environmental assessment. This chapter has raised many concerns and identified a significant number of problems from this situation that perhaps an independent review (audit) body could attempt to solve. Investigation[11] suggests that such an independent organisation could determine the scoping guidelines, referred to as Terms of Reference (TOR), and provide technical advice for the local authority as to the adequacy of the environmental statement. The presence of such independent bodies is a feature of many environmental assessment procedures in other parts of the world and pressure has mounted in the UK to consider such an option although it should be noted that government has yet to support such a proposal.

The Building Intelligence Digest (BID)[15] suggests that the Institute of Environmental Assessment (IEA) would form an ideal national environmental assessment executive should such a move be realised, as it is well structured, can call upon the resources of a considerable number of highly specialised members and ensure a fair balance to environmental and development interests. Such a move, however, may be some years away if at all, but may be a step in the right direction to the development of environmental assessment as a useful concept within construction industry.

References

1   DoE, *Environmental Assessment: A Guide to the Procedures*, HMSO (1989).
2   N. Donlon, *Environmental Impact Assessment*, Research Note No. 92/23, House of Commons Library Research Division (1992).
3   EC, *The Environmental Assessment Directive* on the assessment of the effects of certain public and private projects on the environment: (85/337/EEC), (1985).
4   DoE, *The Town and Country Planning (Assessment of Environmental Effects) Regulations*, HMSO (1988).
5   Scottish Office, *The Environmental Assessment (Scotland) Regulations*, HMSO (1988).
6   Northern Ireland Office, *The Planning (Assessment of Environmental Effects) Regulations (Northern Ireland)*, HMSO (1989).
7   DoE, *Environmental Assessment*, HMSO Explanatory Leaflet (1989).
8   Health and Safety Commission, *The Management of Health and Safety at Work Regulations*, HMSO (1992).
9   C. Jones and C. Wood, *Maintaining Environmental Assessment and Planning*, HMSO (1991).
10 T. Coles, et al., *Practical Experience of Environmental Assessment in the UK*, Institute of Environmental Assessment, Technical Report (1992).
11 V. Weatherall, 'Operation of the UK's Environmental Assessment System: Is There a Need for Modification?', BSc Degree Thesis, Heriot-Watt University, unpublished.
12 K. Fieldhouse, 'Question Time', *Landscape Design* (journal of the Landscape Institute) March edition (1993).
13 T. Coles, and K. Fuller, *Analysis of the Environmental Impact Assessment Market in the UK*, IEA Technical Report (1990).
14 CPRE, *Mock Directive*, Council for Protection of Rural England (CPRE) (1992).
15 BID, 'Planners Poised for Quality Crackdown' *BID Digest*, 1.3 (1981).

7 Environmental Management: Its Application to Briefing, Design and Contract Administration

7.1 Introduction

General

Clearly, environmental management cannot and will not happen by itself. Effective environmental management can only be realised if the many and diverse factors contributing to the construction process are consciously brought together and, moreover, the various building professionals involved perceive the need for environmental management with integrity and commitment. The plain fact is that whilst some aspects of environmental management are imposed by regulation, many aspects rely upon voluntary implementation by informed clients, responsible designers and specifiers and responsive contractors. It is the responsibility of all parties, acting individually and in combination, to ensure that the basic requirements for effective environmental management are met. This chapter addresses the contributions towards environmental management that may be made during the briefing, design and contract administration phases of the construction project process.

Project phases and elements

Following the 'development process' and once planning approval has been given, activity focuses upon the 'construction project process'. This naturally divides into three principal phases with further sub-division into specific elements of activity. Environmental management and its systems, in different ways and stimulated by different contractual parties, has an important contribution to make during each main phase.

The principal phases and sub-divisions of the construction project process are:

(i) Briefing.
(ii) Design – Scheme design
      – Detail design (including specifying).
(iii) Construction (or Contract Administration).

The client's aims

The overall aim of any construction project is:

the design and construction of a building or structure to meet the specific requirements of the client.

In relation to environmental management, the basic requirement will become all the more demanding with those aspects intended to address environmental protection identified and considered during the development phase. Environmental assessment of a proposed project may have identified aspects that will play a significant part in the formulation of the brief, in the design or in the construction process on site. The client's main initial aim is to accurately translate those environmental aspects identified in the development process, and which are important to the client, into an effective project brief from which a basis of ideas can be generated for the design phase.

The basic requirements

Effective environmental management throughout any construction project is dependent upon:

- The client clearly understanding, defining and communicating the environmental requirements for the project during the briefing phase.
- The lead consultant, usually the designer, in association with other consultants, accurately translating the client's environmental needs within the project situation, form and function during the design phase.
- The main contractor, and sub-contractors under the contractor's control, having empathy for environmental management aspects incorporated in the design and translating the design concept into the physical building form, whilst also having environmental sympathy in site activity and respect for the project's environs and populace.

The importance of the client's role

Difficulties are likely to arise where an environmentally sympathetic attitude and approach is not demonstrated at the start of the project process phase. For this reason, if no other, the initial impetus and commitment must come from the client. Where a client is environmentally aware, as indeed many larger developers and clients are today, then the environmental ethos will have been encapsulated in the intra-organisational system and clearly reflected in the development process through the use of environmental assessment. This internal commitment will then filter down through the design and construction processes through the client's choice of designer, materials suppliers and contractors. Where such awareness and intent is lacking however, there can be little expectation of environmental management gathering serious momentum through the isolated efforts of others. Environmental management is essentially a team effort and commitment that must be led by the client. It must continue the initial interest and stimulus from the environmental assessment process through design and into construction activity on site.

Environmental management systems

Where participants to the construction process are part of an organisation that utilises a formalised systems management approach, such as large contractors for example, the basic framework and structure for environmental management will have been engendered at organisational level, and therefore it is a case of transferring those intra-organisational concepts to implementation at project site level. What is needed therefore are management techniques to identify the potential environmental effects of activity and management mechanisms to ensure that these effects are prevented or mitigated effectively and efficiently when they do occur in the project based processes.

Management mechanisms

An important mechanism in the practice of environmental management and one which recurs throughout the project based processes, although taking a diverse stance at different phases and undertaken by different parties, is that of the environmental site survey (ESS). This mechanism, a somewhat natural extension, in principle, to the environmental assessment process, enables the designer or contractor to formulate a practical environmental management regime to 'manage' the potential environmental effects of activities as they occur in the design or construction oriented workplace. It is the continuity of effort to, first, employ an investigative mechanism, the environmental site survey, to identify potential environmental effects of activity, and second, to implement monitoring and control systems to manage activity, upon which environmental management across the project is determined in practice.

Cost implications

It would be a fallacy to suggest that environmental management is achievable without cost. Plainly it is not. There will always be some cost implication to the pursuit of environmental management and this will be borne to a large extent by the client. The essential point is that environmental management must be considered as a project priority along with other project determinants such as time, cost and quality, and 'balanced' with rather than compromised by these factors. Environmental management will, obviously, feature in the tendering process. Prospective contractors will find that the act of environmental management on site is not inexpensive and the cost of control mechanisms used will need to be incorporated in the tender build-up. If environmental management forms a written part of the project specification for the designer and has been costed in the bid by the contractor then there is much greater likelihood that environmental management practices will be encouraged in the project process phase.

Reviewing environmental management in the briefing, design and contract administration process

Although environmental management must follow environmentally sympathetic professional practices by all the project participants to have overall effectiveness, the genuine contribution will vary across the different project phases. For any sense to be gleaned of the contribution that can be made by environmental management, the phases of the construction project process must be looked at individually so that concepts and practices can be identified and reviewed. The environmental management inputs throughout the construction process are reflected in Figure 7.1.

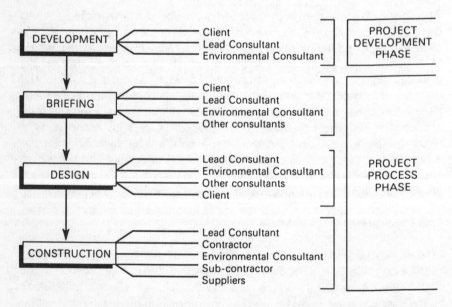

Figure 7.1   Environmental management inputs to the construction process

7.2 The briefing phase

General

Briefing is a crucial activity that begins the construction process in real terms. An accurate and effective brief is essential for, first, translating those environmentally sympathetic aspects identified in environmental assessment, and second, for laying the groundwork for an effective design phase. Briefing, in a conventional construction situation, can be a difficult task and it is made all the more problematic when environmental demands are additionally placed upon it. The principal cause of difficulty in the briefing process is invariably one of information provision and communications management – more specifically, the difficulties of handling large amounts of information; information coming from many different participants simultaneously; the correct interpretation of communication between the parties; even the evolving pattern of the briefing process does not lend itself to accurate perception and projection of project information. These aspects in themselves are difficult to manage and are made all the more fraught as environmental management aspects, which are at this stage only anticipated and not confirmed, are postulated for consideration in the briefing process. The client is essentially 'at the helm' in the early part of the briefing phase. Unfortunately, the client is not involved solely with this process but is rather more extensively involved in a great many other project interests which may deflect him from the important task of briefing.

Aims of the briefing phase

The principal aims of the briefing phase with regard to environmental management are to:

(i) Accurately translate the likely environmental effects of the project identified in environmental assessment during the development phase into mitigating measures in the brief for design and construction.

(ii) Ensure that the environmental aspects identified in (i) above are balanced practically with client expectations, bias and important project criteria such as time, cost and quality.

(iii) Provide the designer with an outline set of client needs and specifications that take in those environmental aspects within design options, situation, form and function, i.e. within layout; use; performance; style; configuration; etc.

The tasks involved

The main tasks of the briefing phase, within which environmental management must be considered, are as follows:

- Appointment of consultants.
- Feasibility study.
- Site investigation.
- Development of outline brief.
- Cost assessment.
- Consideration of procurement route, contract forms and team selection.
- Development of final brief.

Likely problems

For reasons already mentioned and others that will become evident, the briefing process may not always run smoothly and a number of problems may be experienced when incorporating environmental management aspects within the brief. These include:

- Environmental concepts may not have been adequately identified and considered in environmental assessment, leading to a lack of information for use in the briefing phase.
- The client may not fully understand the environmental effects of the project and not appreciate their real implications upon the design and, subsequently, the construction phase of the development.
- The client may lose sight of the environmental orientation in attempting to meet other seemingly more pressing project criteria such as performance characteristics, and configuration or standards of finish, for example.
- The client may through desire or lack of knowledge simply assume a passive role and rely upon the designer to accommodate environmental aspects within the building and its environs, yet the designer's view may not be the same as that of the client.

It is clearly evident that likely problems, in the main, result from a lack of information, misinterpretation of information and inaccurate translation of the client's requirements. The briefing phase therefore is fundamentally concerned with the concept of communication and its flow, with considerable responsibility for its success resting with the client.

The role of the client

The briefing phase is fundamentally concerned with the role of the client. Whilst it is appreciated that the client's initial role is nearly always taken over and influenced by the lead consultant early on, the client should retain sufficient control to guide the briefing process, if his needs and requirements are to be addressed. The client should be able to make decisions from the outset and act quickly and positively to ensure that his genuine environmental needs are satisfied. This can only be achieved if the client is actually involved in the process from project commencement. Of course, many clients sit back and let themselves be guided by the designer. This is perfectly acceptable if the designer is environmentally aware and sympathetic and knows clearly from the environmental statement what the implications to the project are, but it is possible that the designer will not. The impetus must come from the client. The client, particularly if it is a large organisation, may well have in-house expertise and this will make the environmental briefing process easier to undertake.

Influence of the lead consultant

It is easy for the client to be swayed from the desired environmental orientation if the lead consultant takes control away from the client. If total control is assumed by the lead consultant, then undoubtedly the determinants of cost, time and quality are likely to predominate. For this reason, if no other, the client should take responsibility to impress the importance of the environmental perspective for the project along with other important criteria. These criteria should be evaluated in the same light, be determined clearly and be agreed upon by the client and lead consultant. The lead consultant thereafter is concerned not with the importance of the environmental aspect because it is already established but rather is concerned with accommodating it on balance with those factors which must be considered.

Contribution of the environmental consultant

To alleviate the potential difficulties raised between the client and lead consultant, the client may decide to appoint the services of an environmental consultant, probably the same consultant who conducted the environmental assessment at the development phase. This provides for the essential continuity between the development process and the project process. In this way, the task of translating the client's environmental orientation from the environmental statement to the briefing phase should become much easier. It was identified in the preceding chapter that many clients are, in fact, adopting a project management approach to environmental management with the environmental consultant playing a significant part, either taking the lead or working closely with the design consultant. The environmental consultant plays an important role in ensuring that the brief reflects the genuine concerns for environmental effects on the project. The environmental consultant can also provide further continuity to the project process with involvement in the scheme design, detail design and representing the client's environmental position throughout the site works. It is seen as somewhat essential that the client appoints an environmental consultant to work in association with the design consultant at an early stage in the project process.

Practical contribution

It is all too easy to suggest that the client should be involved from the outset, be pro-active and support environmental aspects of the project, but there will be, without doubt, a practical compromise to make in the thinking process. There are increasingly complex environmental arguments put before any client in the normal course of events, even to the most discerning clients. The client may wish to be environmentally sympathetic, particularly if it is a large organisation that is well versed in the use of environmental management systems. The client may well have long-term vision to see potential benefits and future needs, but it is still highly likely that the client will be compromised by the cost implications of practical environmental management in the project. There will certainly be some trade-off between the desire to be environmentally friendly in the brief and the importance given to cost, time and project quality. Again, when legislation is a great influence to the client's organisation or activities, environmental management is likely to predominate, but where it is not, then environmental management is simply the choice of the client. It is up to the client to decide just what priority he places upon environmental management and how much he is prepared to support its implementation when drawing together the brief.

The importance of communication, control of information and feedback

There is little doubt that communication, control of information and its feedback is essential to the briefing phase, quite simply because briefing is heavily dependent upon information. Feedback of information is particularly significant since ideas from many contributors will form the basis of the final brief and these must be drawn together in a clear and coherent form that is understandable and agreeable to the client. Again, this is an aspect which is perhaps best overseen by the lead consultant working closely with the environmental consultant who can ensure that environmental aspects are fully incorporated as the lead consultant brings the brief towards its final content and form. See Figure 7.2.

Briefing: action by the client

The client can play an significant part in the briefing process by:

- Becoming actively involved from the outset.
- Taking a prominent stance in briefing procedures and tasks.
- Demonstrating commitment to environmental aspects of the project.

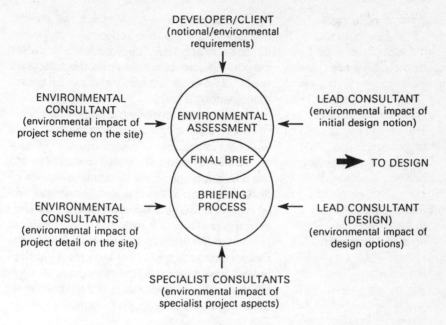

Figure 7.2   Input of information to production of final brief

- Ensuring continuity of environmental orientation from the 'development' phase into the 'project process' phase.
- Appointing a specialist environmental consultant (outside the role of the design consultant) to safeguard environmental interests and orientation of the project.

Within the various stage tasks of the briefing process, the client should:

- In feasibility study: identify clearly the environmental orientation of the project in relation to the project's general aims, objectives, resources, and pattern of management.

- In the outline brief: emphasise the environmental orientation established in environmental assessment for analysis by the appointed consultant.

- In the appointment of consultants: appoint an environmental consultant specifically to oversee the project's environmental orientation and select the lead consultant (perhaps even at the suggestion of the environmental consultant) who will best serve the environmental aims on balance with other project priorities.

- In considering procurement route, contract form and team selection: choose the procurement route that best meets the environmental orientation. (A non-traditional approach may be preferable.) This will have an obvious influence upon the organisation of design, construction and construction management.

- In cost assessment: budget for environmental management within the cost outline target as some additional cost will be inevitable.

- In site investigation: consolidate the investigations undertaken at the environmental assessment stage with additional information from the designer and an environmental site survey conducted by the environmental consultant.

- In the final brief: draw together the environmental information for inclusion with other detailed aspects of the project. The environmental standpoint at this time forms the entire basis of the environmental orientation of the design process.

7.3   The design phase

General

The design phase is naturally divided into two distinct but clearly related elements, these being:

(i) Scheme design.
(ii) Detail design.

Whilst environmental management issues are significant in both scheme design and detail design but have essentially different requirements to satisfy as will become evident, environmental orientation is considerably different between the two design aspects.

Definitions

Scheme design is:

the consideration of the evolving and developing construction form, addressing such aspects as position, layout, shape, size and material constituents, i.e. those aspects that make the product aesthetically and situationally acceptable.

Detail design is:

> *the consideration of technology and structure to create the built form, addressing such aspects as components, materials and the assembly processes, i.e. those aspects that give the product performance and make it technologically acceptable.*

Scheme design

If one thinks of environmental influence upon the construction process, one invariably focuses on scheme design. This is because scheme design must take into account a number of fundamental but very significant environmental and situational factors. These are:

- Siting: the location of the development both in terms of its natural orientation and with regard to its environs and access.
- Orientation: the size and position of the development in relation to the overall expanse of the site.
- Natural and built environment: the existence of natural features and man-made structures in the surrounding environs.
- Topography: the orientation of the development site in terms of its natural form, shape and contours.
- Configuration: the relationship of external and internal form in relation to desired style and layout for use.

Aims of scheme design

The principal aim of scheme design is to take those expectations and requirements specified in the client's brief and relate them directly to the project situation. Scheme design is traditionally therefore the responsibility of the client's lead consultant. In terms of environmental management during the design process the lead consultant is likely to be advised himself by the environmental consultant as previously outlined.

There are essentially four phase tasks within scheme design:

- Review brief.
- Scheme design study.
- Review scheme design.
- Finalise scheme design.

Translating the brief into the scheme design

The principal tasks of scheme design with respect to environmental orientation are:

- Translate the brief into a technical specification for materials, products, components and construction processes which include provision for environmental aspects determined in briefing.
- Ensure that the environmental needs and expectations of the client are met, that the design solution meets with technical and layout requirements and comes within an acceptable cost range.
- Ensure that the design solution is constructable, fit for its intended purpose, has the desired levels of durability, reliability and maintainability and, in so doing, meets all environmental criteria.
- Assign design responsibility to appointed advisors. Environmental management will accommodate specialist input and therefore the client is likely to retain the environmental consultant appointed for development and briefing.

Although all projects are different and must therefore be considered on their own merit, scheme design should encourage some or all of the following environmental aspects.

(i) Effects on land.
- Landscape.
- Topography.
- Stability.
- Soil constitution.
- Mineral resources.
- Soil disposal.

(ii) Effects on water resources.
- Natural drainage.
- Ground water level.
- Water courses.
- Underground water.
- Pollution aspects.

(iii) Effects on atmosphere.
- Emissions.
- Odours.
- Noise.
- Vibration.
- Reflections.

(iv) Effects on ecology.
- Flora and fauna.
- Natural habitats.
- Wildlife.
- Ecological balance.

(v) Effects on population.
- Density.
- Proximity.

- Intrusion and disturbance.
- Population change.
- Infrastructure.
- Amenities.

Consideration of these aspects will cover both the primary and secondary effects of the project and consideration must be given to the environmental effects of the development both during the construction and when the finished product is operational. Many of these aspects will have been surveyed and analysed as part of the developer's/client's environmental assessment. During scheme design these can be reassessed as part of the scheme design study.

The aforementioned aspects presuppose that scheme design is concerned only with the siting and orientation of development within its environment. Scheme design is also concerned with the layout and configuration of the internal aspects of the project, as in the case of a building for example. Scheme design, therefore, should address: internal allocations of space; space utilisation; occupation and usage. These aspects form an important part of scheme design, in particular the propensity of the occupants and the activities within the building to affect the environment.

Scheme design study

Scheme design will call upon that information generated by the environmental assessment at the development phase, supplemented by an environmental site survey conducted by the environmental consultant and designer. This will ensure that the potential environmental effects of the project are identified and considered before the client is committed to the detail of the project. Scheme design study provides useful information to both the scheme design and detail design and is an important part of the on-going design review procedure as the information gathered at this stage reinforces aspects considered in the brief.

Scheme design review

Periodic reappraisal of the scheme design is essential in order to ensure that the design continues to meet all the specified requirements and client needs. There are always likely to be changing aspects within design as more information is generated and applied to the project situation. Contract review is therefore essential to the early design processes. It is not uncommon for the brief to be weak in some cases and this can go undetected until information is reviewed during scheme design. It is likely that only such weaknesses in the scheme design resulting from an inadequate brief will be, in fact, the result of deficiencies in the original environmental assessment.

Likely problems

Despite the periodic review of the scheme design, aspects may still go wrong. The main problems are likely to be:

- Scheme design relates the overall orientation of the development to environmental impact and this is often very subjective in nature. It is not always easy to see the potential environmental effects upon the project situation or environs with a high degree of accuracy before they occur.
- Unless firm commitment is reached in the environmental orientations of specific aspects of the project, it is easy for aspects to be changed or lost intentionally or unintentionally at the detail design stage.
- Frequently the environmental orientation is lost through change brought about in the building process on site or by the user in occupation of the development because these aspects are not addressed at all at this stage in the project process.

Scheme design: action by the design consultant

The designer makes a significant contribution to environmental management in the scheme design by:

- Actively translating the client's brief into outline drawings, specifications and contract documentations which include the required environmental consideration.
- Maintaining on-going review of the scheme design process to ensure any environmental weaknesses are alleviated before the final scheme design is presented.
- Systematically considering the project requirements in relation to the significant environmental aspects identified before and during the process.
- Working closely with the environmental consultant to ensure that the above are confirmed.

Within the various stage tasks of scheme design, the designer should:

- In reviewing the brief: ensure all information is clear, understandable and available to the scheme design process.
- In scheme design study: consolidate the information on potential environmental impact identified in environmental assessment and the brief, with information derived from a detailed environmental site survey.

- In scheme design review: ensure periodic review to assess, on an on-going basis, the scheme design to pick up any deficiencies left over from the briefing phase.
- In finalising the scheme design: ensure that all environmental aspects have been enveloped within the scheme design for transfer to the detail design phase.

Detail design

General

Whilst scheme design was identified as being concerned with the developing construction form in relation to its environmental situation, detail design focuses upon the technological aspects of that form. See Figure 7.3. Detail design is therefore mainly concerned with the determination of structure, materials and fabric elements and are encompassed in the following aspects:

- The physical properties of the construction elements that make up the building or structure.
- The construction or assembly implications of the above.
- The conditions of use, given the environment both outside and inside the building.

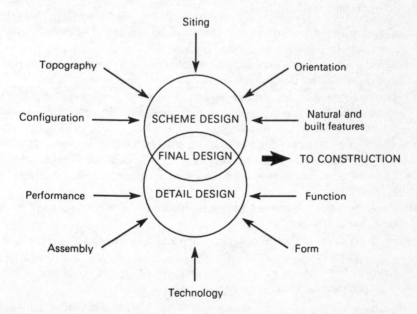

Figure 7.3   Environmental considerations within the design process

Whilst it may be thought that detail design has little or no real interrelationship with environmental issues in the same way that scheme design has, this would be understating its contribution. Environmental management does play an important part in specific aspects of the detailed design undertaking.

The aim of detail design

The principal aims of the detail design element are to:

- Translate the scheme (outline) design specification into detailed and workable design concepts.
- Ensure that the above are developed with due regard to the environmental orientation of the project described in the brief.
- In achieving the above, to ensure that these aspects are incorporated where appropriately in the final design and reflected in documentation which goes out to tender.

There are four main phase tasks within detail design formulation. These are:

- Detail design study.
- Consideration of alternatives.
- Drawing up and documenting.
- Verification and final detail design.

In considering environmental issues within these phase tasks, the designer should undertake the following:

- Develop those environmental ideas generated in the scheme design towards fully detailed design elements.
- Investigate 'green' or eco-design and construction approach as an integral aspect of the design task.
- Ensure that detail design leads to comprehensive and complete project documentation, specifications and drawings incorporating specified environmental performance criteria.
- Consider all statutory legislative requirements relating to environmental management in construction (health and safety, pollution, land use, etc.).
- Evaluate eco-materials and components for potential inclusion in the final design.
- Consider value for money, balancing environmental management with other project priorities.
- Establish detail design review procedures to appraise design progress on an on-going basis.
- Control the various interfaces within the design process, i.e. client/ designer, designer/environmental consultant, etc.

The detail design phase integrates and consolidates the scheme design through the production of the detailed design drawings, specifications and contract documentation. During the detail design phase, the philosophy towards environmental management is clearly established through developing an environmental management design plan that takes into account the basic environmental position of the client and extends this to address how environmental management can become an integral and practical part of the construction phase.

The environmental aspects that may be considered within the detail design phase include:

- Use of 'green' materials (eco-specifying).
- Energy considerations (eco-architecture).
- Waste management.
- Pollution control.
- Health and Safety.

Some of these aspects will essentially be governed by legislation, for example pollution and health and safety aspects, but others will be open to the personal consideration of the designer for example the specification of 'green' materials. Environmental management in detail design, therefore, is very much dependent upon the designer activity seeking to explore an environmentally positive option.

Likely problems

Particular problems are likely to be encountered in the pursuit of environmental management at or following the detail design phase. These include:

- Little may be known of the performance of many eco-materials so their inclusion within the detail design is not without considerable risk.
- New legislation in this area, for example in health and safety management, is not widely understood at this time.
- The ultimate end user of the building is not involved at all in the design phase and yet it is they who determine the realistic quality of fitness for purpose.
- Details incorporated into the design are likely to be compromised during the construction process or by the user so the detailed design can easily lose its environmental orientation.

Detail design: action by the designer

At the detail design stage, the designer should seek to:

- Actively translate the scheme design into detailed design elements.
- Consider the detail design requirements in relation to the environmental aspects identified.

- Monitor on-going review of the design process to ensure all the identified aspects are incorporated.
- Ensure that legislation is met and specified, where appropriate, to document for the construction phase.

Within the various stage tasks of detail design, the designer should:

- In detail design study: ensure that the client's desired environmental and/or user requirements are met.
- In considering alternatives: determine that the most appropriate design is achieved for the design options available.
- In detailing drawings,   ensure that the client's end needs are specifications, and contract   accurately implemented in all contract documentation: documentation.
- In finalising detail design: ensure that the design meets all requirements and that the client is ready to commit to the construction phase.

7.4   The construction phase: contract administration

General

The construction phase of the building process is principally concerned with contract administration and therefore environmental management during this phase is chiefly the responsibility of the main contractor, overseen by the client's lead consultant and other appointed representatives, such as a clerk of works, on site. The contractor plays a very significant role in environmental management and has the opportunity to bring together the environmental desires of the client and designer through the physical construction processes on site.

Environmental management in contract administration involves a three-stage process for the main contractor:

(i) Environmental Appraisal: concerned with the pre-construction period between tender and commencement on site. Linked to the tendering process and site investigation, the purpose of this stage is to identify and appraise the potential environmental effects of site activity.

(ii) Environmental   concerned with start on site and invol-
     Familiarisation: ves the initial site tour to familiarise the contractor's management team with

the project site and take cognisance of the potential for environmental effects of site activity in the workplace.

(iii) Environmental Management and Control: concerned with implementing the necessary control mechanisms to ensure that the potential environmental effects are prevented or when they do occur to 'manage' them through the implementation of an environmental management system.

The aim of environmental management in contract administration

If the contractor has an environmental management system within its organisation then this will have already established the situation for environmental management within the management process, and therefore the primary aim for the contractor will be to transfer the system concepts to management mechanisms on site by which environmental measures can be pursued. This involves the three stages identified. The site structure and organisation of the contractor's environmental management system should present the formal procedure within which the environmental protection measures demanded by the client can be achieved.

Likely reasons for difficulty

The reasons for a contractor failing to meet the demands of environmental management specified by the client are likely to be inadequacies in one or more of the following:

- The clarity of environmental information provided to the contractor in the contract documentation.
- The standards of measures prescribed.
- The definition of environmental priority in relation to other project criteria.

These can be traced to the level of information given to the contractor in the specification and contract documentation. In addition, contractors can create difficulties for themselves through inadequacies in:

- The definitions of environmental responsibility assigned to site supervisors.
- The explanation of environmental protection measures given to site supervising personnel.
- The quality of first-line management and supervision on site and the inspection and control procedures adopted.

The reasons for the presence of these likely problems are not simple. Not only is environmental management dependent upon control of the technical concepts in the project but it is also heavily influenced by human factors. Inadequacies in practical site environmental management could result from poor communications, inadequate interpretation of requirements, a lack of environmental knowledge or simply intransigence by the workforce. It is difficult to pin problems down. Environmental management is dependent upon a sound socio-technical organisational approach. Even when the contractor's organisation has an environmental management system it should not be taken for granted that management or the workforce, i.e. the 'operational' staff, are completely conversant with the environmental management demands, because each site is different, staffing is different and effectively each site is a new situation. Education and training is therefore important for both management and the workforce.

Likewise, communication and information flow is essential to the success of environmental management. A regime must be initiated that clearly identifies where the potential environmental problems of the project are, how they will be managed and who is responsible for their management. These require the consideration of practical measures at pre-construction and during the construction phase.

Pre-construction

During the pre-construction phase between tender and commencement on site the contractor should undertake the following:

- Review carefully the client's environmental management requirements as specified in the contract documents.
- Attend pre-contract meetings and address specifically all aspects of environmental management relating to the site processes.
- Approve the contractor's own organisational environmental management system in relation to those aspects identified.

During construction

A number of these aspects relate to little more than good sound site practice but they are nonetheless essential to effective environmental management at project level. The contractor should ensure that he:

- Provides a well-structured and organised approach to site organisation.
- Clearly determines the requirements of environmental management and assigns responsibility to site personnel.
- Constantly monitors environmental management aspects on site in a systematic way and records all environmental issues.

- Constantly liaises with the client/designer/environmental consultant to ensure continued sound environmental practices.
- Provides a formalised system of deliveries for environmentally sensitive resources including appropriate storage, protection and distribution on site.

The contractor's environmental site survey

To achieve effective environmental management at both the pre-construction and construction stages a management mechanism should be employed to satisfy the requirements of environmental appraisal and environmental familiarisation and provide the informative basis for environmental management at site level. The principal mechanism for achieving this is the contractor's environmental site survey. This is a two-stage process of identification and appraisal of issues and familiarisation with these issues in the workplace, and these two stages quite naturally lead into the implementation of the environmental management system itself on site.

The aim of the environmental site survey is to make a first-hand assessment of the potential sources of environmental impact on the project site and provide the basis for planning and implementing the environmental management system at site level.

For all potential environmental effects, the environmental site survey is concerned with:

- Identification and awareness.
- Analysis.
- Review.
- Communication.
- Control.

Prior to commencement on site, the objective is to make site management fully aware of the potential for environmental effect of project activities. Building on the tender site investigation, the contractor should identify and confirm all potential sources of environmental effect for his intended activities, operatives and procedures. Information gathered should be analysed to consider and plan preventive control procedures for 'managing' the anticipated environmental effects.

Immediately upon commencement on site, an on-site appraisal tour should be made, led by the site manager with all supervisory personnel. The aim is to familiarise them with the planned works and take note of the likely effects of site activity identified.

The contractor's environmental site survey should systematically identify to management those aspects of site activity which will have a significant potential to affect the site and its environs. These include, for example: spillages; discharges; contamination; and forms of pollution. Once identified, the contractor will be in a position to plan, monitor and control for those environmental effects to ensure that they are prevented, or where they do occur, are minimised, i.e. implement the environmental management system on site.

Considerable information will, of course, have come from the contractor's pre-tender site visit and, in addition, information should be available from the client's environmental assessment report and consultant's design data. All these sources should be reviewed before commencement on site. Some of the potential environmental effects will be subject to legislative control and therefore the contractor is bound to mitigate their manifestation. Further aspects will be covered by the client's specification requirements and therefore must also be actively addressed. Other aspects should form part of the contractor's voluntary attempt to protect the environmental in the course of good site practice. Where this latter aspect is concerned much is dependent upon the discretion of the contractor's and the quality of his construction practices.

The key project areas for environmental management application by the contractor

In meeting the environmental needs of the client, environmentally related legislation and good on-site construction practices, the contractor should address a number of key project areas. These should have been identified clearly in the contractor's environmental site survey. These are:

- Atmospheric emissions.
- Discharges and spillages.
- Waste management.
- Handling hazardous substances.
- Discharges to water.
- Health and safety aspects.

These risk areas may be evaluated in one of two ways, by:

(i) Route of emission; air, water, land etc.
(ii) Environmental effect of activity, or at location: storage areas, plant fuelling bunds, toilet blocks etc.

Environmental management: action by the contractor

Two aspects are highly significant and should be determined by the contractor. These are, to develop:

(i) An Environmental Management Plan: to provide systematic mechanisms for identifying and managing the key projects areas listed (atmosphere emissions; discharge and spillage etc.), i.e. management of the 'technical' aspects.

(ii) A Health and Safety Management Plan: to provide systematic mechanisms for managing all aspects of health and safety on the project (employees and the public), i.e. management of the 'human' aspect.

The contractor's environmental management plan

The contractor's environmental site survey will have identified the potential for environmental effects on site from construction activity and brought them to the attention of supervisory management and the workforce. Using the organisation environmental management system as the framework, the contractor should transfer and apply these principles in the site-based processes through the project environmental management plan. This plan should develop its approach through three principal areas of consideration:

(i)   Specify requirements.
(ii) Assign responsibilities.
(iii) Implement mechanisms.

Requirements

In each area of site activity the contractor should ensure that:

- The potential for environmental effects is clearly identified.
- There are planned controls to prevent the environmental effects occurring.
- There is a course of action to 'manage' the environmental effect should it occur.
- There is an active monitoring procedure to indicate if harmful environmental effects occur.
- Action is implemented quickly and effectively to mitigate any environmental effect.
- All environmental effects are systematically recorded, together with any resources taken in mitigation.
- Environmental situations are reviewed to determine cause, the effectiveness of actions taken and the project environmental management plan updated.

Responsibilities

It is the responsibility of supervisory management to ensure that the above requirements are met by employing systematic mechanisms that:

- Makes all personnel aware of the potential for environmental effect and impressing upon them the need to report 'any' breach of environmental integrity, however small.
- Ensures recorded daily checks in all vital areas of site activity.

- Reviews daily checking procedures at weekly site meetings.
- Collates weekly data for discussions at monthly project meetings.
- Information is collated for long-term performance review.

Mechanisms

Simple site reporting mechanisms such as pro-forma checklists should be adopted to formally record:

- Occurrences of a potentially harmful environmental effect.
- The location of the problem.
- Reason for its occurrence.
- Any action taken.
- Review to see if action has been effective.
- Further action needed.
- That an incident report has been made (where an environmental effect is notifiable to a regulatory body, to ensure that this has been undertaken).

Environmental management case study: contracting organisation

Positive steps to introduce an environmental management plan were illustrated in the site-based procedures of one contracting organisation. Focusing upon specific site activities and their potential environmental effects, waste management, pollution mitigation and contamination controls were adopted. Within these aspects, potential dangers were identified, for example routes of emission of substance spillage and wastage of bulk materials. Their levels of importance were then classified and priority areas for management attention determined. Throughout the project each aspect was closely monitored and evaluated on a continuous basis. On reflection although the contractor could not accurately quantify the potential benefits derived it was suggested that, in his experience, there had been fewer instances of having to address particular problems, for example complaints relating to site noise, construction traffic leaving mud on the public highway. In addition, although there had been several instances of oil and diesel spillage on the site exit road these had been dealt with promptly through the environmental monitoring procedures. Waste management was shown to be advantageous as, again in his experience, it was felt there had been less general material wastage because of the greater consideration given to that aspect.

Environmental management case study: interdisciplinary design-build organisation

BS 7750 encourages organisations to undertake an environmental review of their activities and to identify areas that may be improved. One design-build organisation illustrated this aspiration in an internal environmental review of their activities.

The organisation examined ways in which their organisational performance could be enhanced both at the design stage and during the construction stage of a construction project. It was determined that a much closer relationship should be established with some of their clients as this had proved a stumbling block on previous projects. Similarly, a set of better guidelines for working through the design stage was considered which would systematically consider environmental aspects as the design evolved. Having considered the major environmental aspects throughout the development process it proved much easier, as one might expect given the design-build orientation, to follow environmental issues through to the construction phase on site. The organisation suggested that environmental management systems are likely to be much more effective where a non-traditional design-build contract is used as environmental management can be one of a number of primary issues brought sharply into focus.

The contractor's health and safety management plan

It was identified in Chapter 5 that EC Directives, effective from 1993, have placed new and considerable obligations upon contractors with regard to the management of health and safety on construction sites. The focus of regulations encompassed by these Directives is to make the workplace or the temporary construction site, and also its environs, a safe and healthy environment and to uphold the safety of both employees on the site and the public affected by the site. For details of the EC Directive and its associated statutory legislative requirements the reader is directed to Chapter 5.

To accommodate these Directives, the contractor should develop a formalised health and safety management plan (contingent with that developed by the Planning Supervisor on behalf of the client) for each construction project based upon the policy and framework for health and safety existing within the organisation. As with the environmental management plan, the health and safety plan should be formulated around the three core elements:

(i)   Requirements.
(ii) Responsibilities.
(iii) Mechanisms.

Requirements

Requirements for the management of health and safety are specified under current regulations as follows:

- To implement the planning supervisors' health and safety plan for the project.

- To update this plan as required throughout the project.
- To accommodate health and safety management between contractors on the project.

Responsibilities

The contracting organisation, through the site manager, should ensure that the following are enveloped within the project's health and safety management plan:

- All potential risks and hazards associated with site activity are clearly identified (e.g. handling of hazardous materials; use of safety equipment, etc.).
- Responsibilities for the above are assigned to particular personnel.
- All responsibilities are overseen by the site manager, or on larger sites by a designated health and safety officer.
- Monitoring mechanisms are in place to identify problems arising in the recognised risk areas.
- Planned actions are implemented when the integrity of such aspects is breached.
- All incidents are described in project and statutory records.
- The necessity of further action is considered.
- Records are maintained for safety performance evaluation and auditing at organisational level.

These responsibilities, at project level, are in addition to the statutory obligations of the contractor at company organisational level, e.g. health and safety policy, notices, provisions, etc.

Mechanisms

The same mechanisms that were postulated for the environmental management plan may be implemented for health and safety management. The accent is upon keeping the on-site mechanisms clear, simple to understand and easy to use. Mechanisms should formally record:

- Occurrence of health and safety incidents.
- Reason for the occurrence.
- Any action taken.
- Review to see if action has been effective.
- Further action needed.
- That an accident report has been made (where an incident is notifiable to a regulatory body, to ensure that this has been undertaken).

Particular aspects are important to the rigour of the health and safety plan. These are as follows:

- *Risk Assessment*
  The need for risk assessment is becoming an ever more important element within the site process. In health and safety matters, high risk areas should be determined, as in practice they will demand a greater proportion of resources devoted to the monitoring and control mechanisms. By ranking risks, monitoring and control practices can be established and high risk areas be given the attention they deserve. For example, a contractor may identify and rank potential dangers from substances stored on site or ass-ess the potential risk of spillage and anticipate the consequences. More time can then be spent managing those aspects carrying the greater risk.
- *Active Monitoring*
  An active monitoring system is essential to establish the effectiveness of the plan. On-going monitoring provides essential feedback such that the frequency of inspection can be determined on a pro-active basis rather than on a merely routine and perhaps superficial basis.
- *Auditing and Review*
  All control systems demonstrate the tendency to deteriorate over the course of the project. Management mechanisms should therefore be employed which reviews, formally at periodic intervals, health and safety performance on the project such that improvements can be effected in areas of weakness identified.

Environmental management case study: contractor's health and safety plan

Whilst almost all contractors implement a formalised health and safety policy under current legislation, one contractor, seen in compiling case study material, had taken the step towards implementing risk assessment as an intrinsic part of his health and safety consideration. This essentially involved the contractor in undertaking an extensive assessment of risk for the project, prior to commencement on site. Areas of work or activities seen as being potentially hazardous were given particular management attention. In addition, prior to commencement on site all staff and employees were requested to attend a pre-contract site safety induction course to familiarise them with the particular risks attendant to the project.

The contractor reviewed that the induction measures introduced, together with the sound safety procedures they adopted on all sites, served to lessen the degree of on-site risk to their employees, this being reflected in a reduced number of injuries sustained during site activity.

7.5   Environmental management: current concerns and issues

Although there is little empirical data available at this time concerning the implementation of formalised environmental management within construction, research in the course of undertaking this work sought the opinions and views of a number of major client organisations, consultants and contractors with some experience or knowledge of environmental management concepts. The following represents an impression of the concerns and attitudes towards environmental management currently prevalent within the construction process. It is intended to provide a flavour of the varying views held. It looks at a range of views from the perspective of different project participants and those with differing levels of environmental awareness.

Clients

- *A client that has a recognised environmental management system within the organisation is in a much better position to address the environmental issues that arise throughout the construction process:*
  One client organisation said that 'although our corporate policy and strategy towards environmental management was essentially determined by the need for public image and commercial recognition, we had found that a prominent environmental awareness within our organisation placed us in a much better position with respect to the development plan and also the briefing phase of new projects we procured'. It was felt that we would, in the near future, introduce some level of environmental management to all potential projects, where this is felt it might be advantageous.

- *The client should take a prominent role in environmental management matters during both the briefing and design phases:*
  The same client organisation said that 'given the fragmented nature of the construction process in traditional contracting, the only way in which any measure of environmental protection could be assured was for the client to assume the dominant role'. It was currently impractical to consider environmental management as a pre-qualification criteria but a strong environmental stance in briefing and design was seen as most desirable.

- *The appointment of an environmental consultant is seen as essential:*
  Although the clients, in the main, appointed their design/engineering consultants first in the traditional lead consultant role, it was felt that leaving environmental matters to the lead consultant was nowadays impractical on large projects. 'It was expected that the design consultant would employ an environmental consultant if needed as part of a multi-disciplinary design team.' All the client organisations had in-house environmental staff but it was recognised that those tended towards the technological and engineering areas and were not therefore totally suited to the full range of environmental issues that must be addressed today on very high profile commercial projects – for

example: land use; habitat destruction; energy consumption; use of natural resources, etc. It was emphasised, however, that they do have an essential role to play in the environmental evaluation processes from the organisation's viewpoint both prior to and during the project process phase.

- *A holistic and practical view of environmental management is essential:*
  One client organisation suggested that the current emphasis today of attempting to mitigate environmental impact completely was somewhat unrealistic: 'there would always be a price to pay for development and this had to be offset against the potential benefits'. From their point of view, everything that could be done to protect the project environs would be done but not to the detriment of other project priorities. 'Environmental management, like QA for that matter, has to be viewed in the round.'

Consultants

- *Environmental management is assuming greater prominence within the design role:*
  The view was expressed that larger clients, in general, are 'expecting more in the way of environmental consideration from the design process' and that a greater range of environmental issues were being raised than had been the case in the past. In addition, changing legislation was, without doubt, likely to place the designer under greater pressure to consider environmental issues in the design processes although just in what ways and to what extent could not be determined.

- *Briefing is seen to be the key determinant of environmental consideration in the design role:*
  It was clear that briefing is seen to be the keystone of environmental management within the design processes. It is essential for clients to make their views known clearly and early on for this to be incorporated into the brief. One consultant commented that 'there is a wide range of positions among clients from those that are extremely environmentally aware and specify well to those that are really uninformed and rely totally on the architect for advice'.

- *Clients are taking a greater interest and seek more involvement in the briefing and design processes:*
  Consultants serving large clients felt that whilst their role was not being diminished, it is 'certainly the case that clients are more knowledgeable in environmental issues'. Nowadays clients are expecting more on-going involvement in the design process. One consultant

commented that 'it was almost as if the client was checking certain steps with his in-house expertise . . . too much involvement can be off-putting'.

- *There is growing support for multi-disciplinary team approach:*
  It was identified that in recent times the trend towards multi-disciplinary teams for briefing and design was growing. Eventually the range of skills needed to fully appreciate the environmental aspects of some projects is too great for some traditional practices. Design practices therefore are tending to branch out towards environmentally multi-skilled design teams. One design practice suggested that 'amongst those consultants that see themselves moving extensively into environmental assessment and environmental management, it is essential for them to acquire not only design and engineering skills but skills in landscape architecture and ecological issues'. Consultants seek to provide the client with a total environmental package.

Contractors

- *Better environmental performance is being expected of contractors:*
  There were few doubts among the contractors' group that clients were expecting more in the way of environmental performance during site activities, beyond that of merely the minimum expected under legislation. More environmental demands are being seen in contract documentation and site meetings more frequently raised issues of environmental aspects of projects. It was generally felt that 'greater pressure is being exerted and that the future would see this increasing further, an aspect which contractors might not like but have to accept'.

- *Contractors see environmental management systems as being the natural progression of quality systems:*
  Several contractors who used quality systems clearly see environmental management as a natural extension to quality assurance systems in the future. 'Such demands should not tax organisations unduly, if they are well prepared for increasing legislation and client demands in environmental matters, as they can be dealt with through the existing quality system with some reorientation in site procedures.'

- *Environmental management is ostensibly the product of good site management aided by simple and systematic environmental management mechanisms:*
  There is little doubt that 'environmental management on site does not really need any "special" abilities but does require considerable effort and commitment'. Communication is paramount, as are simple

mechanisms, to check, record and review environmental issues on a systematic basis.

- *Health and safety management is becoming more prominent in site organisation and management:*

    It was identified that contractors see their increasing involvement in specific environmental matters, health and safety being the most demanding, and that risk management was becoming inherent in the work processes. Some confusion is apparent, however, as regards the requirements of new legislation and what demands this would actually make upon contractors. Concern was raised over the potential for environmental management issues given the effect of recessionary influences. One contractor commented that: 'Times are hard enough and we (the industry) have only just come to terms with quality assurance. Now it's environmental management. What next?'

8 Environmental Management in Construction: An Overview

8.1 The challenge for environmental management

It is overwhelmingly evident that many organisations in virtually all industrial sectors throughout Europe are incorporating a formal environmental policy as part of their corporate responsibility, indeed some have taken the unprecedented step toward environmental auditing. Notwithstanding, environmental awareness remains at a disturbingly low level within the construction industry. The construction industry has been slow to respond to environmental issues compared with other major industries, both across Europe and particularly in the UK. This seems to demonstrate a somewhat short-term perspective, perhaps waiting for market forces and legislation to determine its interest. With the rapid emergence of increasingly stringent environmental legislation both in the EC and the UK, organisations will find that they simply have to react to changing circumstance. Companies which demonstrate vision and anticipate future environmental demands will be in a position of competitive advantage, able to respond to changing environmental circumstances with greater success.

Much of the current environmental debate is focused upon how construction industry might be encouraged to ensure that its activities are not damaging to the environment. Whilst legislation plays a very significant part, environmental performance is greatly dependent upon the voluntary contribution of construction professionals. The construction industry, therefore, has a very clear choice ahead of it. Does it actively want to participate in environmentally sound construction practices, or does it simply sit back and wait for more stringent regulation to force it into significant action.

8.2 Impetus for change

Research presents some indications that there are changing expectations within the construction industry and that there are clear marketing advantages to be gained by promoting the environmental face of the organisation. Clearly, organisations of all types and within all construction sectors simply cannot ignore the weight of evidence assembled in favour of environmental management. Environmental awareness within the marketplace is, without doubt, a powerful impetus for change. It is influencing some construction oriented organisations to adopt more rigorous environmental standards of performance and increasing the demand for environmentally sympathetic products. As such demands increase so the support for change will become more manifest. Environmental consumerism both within the construction industry, and more generally outside, will become a strong impetus for change in the future.

The construction industry has an undisputed and significant impact on the environment and considerable and lasting change within the industry is necessary if future environmental problems are to be avoided. Such change is, without doubt, both socially desirable and technologically and financially feasible. Whilst construction, at this time, appears to have a very short-term view of environmental impact, stricter legislation can only determine that it acts responsibly not only in the short term but in the long term. The construction industry therefore must be ready to address the challenge of environmental management.

8.3 The current position

It is clearly evident in some EC member countries, and even as far afield as the USA and Japan, that the early establishment of environmental regulation has given their industries commercial advantage in the world marketplace. Companies in those countries have a tangible headstart in environmental management as legislation begins to tighten around the world. As construction industry will undoubtedly face tougher standards, it will be those organisations who support environmental management and utilise environmental management systems who can best respond to the demands and who will be the most successful.

The introduction of the EC Directive on environmental assessment in the late 1980s has impressed upon the construction industry in the UK the need for greater environmental awareness by all construction professionals and the adoption of a more pro-active approach towards environmental management. The implementation of this initiative has not been trouble-free however, leading one to question if environmental assessment within the UK construction industry has been an early success. Similarly, the concept of environmental management and implementation of environmental management systems, whilst making sound practical sense, is meeting considerable early scepticism within the industry. One must ask if these concepts are, first, properly benefiting the UK construction industry and, second, where are they likely to lead to in the future.

8.4   Environmental assessment: is it protecting the environment?

Environmental assessment is essentially a management tool to assist decision makers, ensuring that the potential environmental impact of a proposed development is fully appreciated before the project is awarded planning permission. In this way, environmental assessment makes a significant contribution to environmental protection. As a result of environmental assessment, some proposals are amended, indicating that environmental issues are duly considered and that some measure of protection is afforded. However, it is not a requirement that projects be rejected if environmental assessment identifies adversarial environmental effects. Moreover, it is well appreciated that many larger high-profile construction projects are not subject to environmental assessment, and where projects are, that intended procedures are not always followed. In addition, whilst it is possible to address the limited environmental impact of proposals as they progress through the environmental assessment process, many wider environmental issues go unchallenged.

The provision of accurate and unambiguous information is a clear advantage to the development decision-making process. The principal concern of the environmental assessment process currently is that many environmental statements accepted by planning authorities as acceptable are, in fact, of very dubious quality. This problem arises, in the main, from the general lack of awareness for the process by both developers and planning authorities alike. Producing a good quality environmental statement should benefit both the developer and the environment. If environmental assessment forms an integral part of project formulation it should actively aid both the briefing and design processes. It should postulate better environmental options for using the finished product and lead to alternative processes in construction which are both more time and cost effective. In addition, an effective environmental assessment and a good quality environmental statement can help allay the understandable fear that is often held by the public through the lack of information. Some suggest that public consultation has yet to be fully integrated into the development process such that the public who exist in the environment and even the environment itself only play a marginal role to development intent within the current environmental assessment process.

The current criticisms are that environmental assessment may appear to have little effect on the decision-making process; have few tangible benefits; be poorly carried out; and offer insufficient opportunity for public involvement, but it will assume a greater role in the future. In so doing, environmental assessment can raise general environmental awareness, provide for a more informed and improved decision-making process and be an integral and important aspect of project development, briefing, design and construction. With improvement, environmental assessment can become a very significant element in the future of environmental protection.

8.5 Environmental management: its realisation

In the same way that environmental assessment has met with a certain degree of scepticism within the construction industry, so too has the concept of environmental management and the implementation of environmental management systems. Early scepticism is not unexpected, however, and environmental management appears to be mirroring the evolutionary development of quality assurance, seen in the mid to late 1980s. Environmental management is essentially an organisation's response to its environmental situation in the course of its business, and is likely to develop to be a prominent issue within the construction industry in the future. In the immediate to short term, interest will focus upon newly introduced environmentally related legislation supported by voluntary participation by construction professionals, whilst in the longer term there is likely to be an expansion of requirements but invoked by mandatory legislation.

There is little doubt that construction organisations, like businesses in most all commercial and industrial sectors, face increasing pressure from investors, clients, regulatory bodies and the public in relation to their environmental performance. Compliance with environmental standards is already seen as a pre-qualification criteria in specific situations and this is likely to proliferate with environmental requirements, of some kind, to be met by all construction professionals, suppliers and service organisations.

It has been clearly identified that those organisations who adopt environmental management systems are much better placed to accommodate the growing trend towards environmental management. It is these organisations within construction who will best respond to the demands of environmental assessment and auditing, an aspect which will, without doubt, assume considerable significance in the future. The EC Eco-Management and Auditing Scheme (CEMAS) is perhaps the most prominent example, forming the benchmark for environmental performance across Europe. Whilst its introduction was made on a voluntary basis it is likely to become mandatory if organisations should not follow positively.

In addition to the likelihood of increasingly stringent environmental legislation, the consolidation of environmental management and auditing schemes and significant commercial pressures, practical environmental management, at this time, is highly dependent upon the voluntary contribution of construction professionals. It is these professionals who must make environmental management work in the course of the practical construction process, in briefing, design and construction. Whilst tangible criticisms have been raised regarding both the potential of environmental management within the construction process and the fact that it is one of the most challenging aspects for construction industry to address, there is little doubt that a profound change in environmental orientation is ensuing and construction industry must be ready to work within a more demanding operational climate than it has hitherto.

Appendix 1: Definition of Terms

This appendix presents the definition of terms relevant to 'Environmental Management' and 'Environmental Management Systems'. Where referenced, definitions are derived from known authoritative sources. Definitions are sequenced alphabetically, commencing with terms directly prefixed by 'Environment' or 'Environmental'.

Environment:

The environs and conditions in which the organisation exists and functions.

Environmental Assessment (EA) or Environmental Impact Assessment (EIA):

An appraisal technique for ensuring that the potential environmental effects of any new development are identified and considered before any approval is given.

Environmental effect:

The effects of organisational activity upon its environs whether direct or indirect, detrimental or beneficial.

Environmental impact prediction:

The process of assessing the potential for environmental effect of those aspects identified during scoping and baseline studies.

Environmental management:

The aspects of policy, strategy, procedures and practice that form the organisation's response to its environmental situation in the course of its business.

Environmental management audit:

The periodic detailed evaluation of the organisation's environmental management system to determine its effectiveness in satisfying the environmental policy.

Environmental management manual:

The organisation's documentation of procedures and working instructions for implementing the environmental management programme.

Environmental management programme:

The organisational approach to formalising the means of achieving environmental policy, aims and objectives.

Environmental management representative:

A person with defined authority and responsibility for ensuring that the requirements of environmental standards are implemented and monitored.

Environmental management review:

The management evaluation of its environmental system with regard to changing environmental awareness, conditions and legislation.

Environmental management statement:

A public pronouncement by the organisation's board of directors stating the intentions and principles of action of the organisation in respect of potential environmental effects of its business.

Environmental management system:

The organisation's formal structure that implements environmental management.

Environmental monitoring:

The process of monitoring the environmental effects of the project, if and when the project is given approval to proceed.

Environmental policy:

A published statement of organisational intentions in relation to potential environmental effects.

Environmental objectives:

The measurable organisational targets, or goals, for environmental performance.

(Preparatory) environmental review:

The detailed consideration of all aspects of an organisation's business with regard to its environmental situation as a basis for developing an environmental management system.

Environmental Statement (in environmental assessment) (ES):

'A publicly available document setting out the developer's own assessment of the likely environmental effects of his proposed development, which he prepares and submits in conjunction with his planning application.'

Environmental strategy:

The organisation's considered actions in respect of its environmental situation in the formulation of policy, aims and objectives.

Baseline studies:

The identification of the significant environmental impact that must be assessed.

Directive management:

The level of management within the organisation that focuses upon environmental system control.

Mitigation assessment:

The consideration of the measures to be taken to alleviate or minimise environmental effects.

Operational Management:

The level of management within the organisation that focuses upon environmental systems implementation.

Project description (in the environmental statement):

A sufficient and clear description of the project together with details of its location.

Scoping:

The process of directing environmental assessment towards aspects of specific importance.

Screening:

The process of determining, for a particular project, the need for an environmental assessment.

Statutory consultees:

Public bodies with statutory environmental responsibilities who must be consulted by the planning authority when a planning application is considered.

Strategic management:

The level of management within the organisation that focuses upon environmental system policy and development.

Appendix 2: List of UK Statutory Instruments Relevant to Environmental Assessment

The following list presents current environmental assessment legislation in the UK. The list is sub-divided to identify legislation in England, Scotland and Northern Ireland. These Regulations implement the EC Directive on environmental assessment.

EC

- Council Directive 85/337/EEC of 27 June 1985 on the assessment of the effects of certain public and private projects on the environment.

UK

England:

- Town and Country Planning (Assessment of Environmental Effects) Regulations 1988 (SI No. 1199)
- Town and Country Planning (Assessment of Environmental Effects) (Amendment) Regulations 1990 (SI No. 367)
- Environmental Assessment (Afforestation) Regulations 1988 (SI No. 1207)
- Land Drainage Improvement Works (Assessment of Environmental Effects) Regulations 1988 (SI No. 1217)
- Harbour Works (Assessment of Environmental Effects) Regulations 1988 (SI No. 1336)
- Harbour Works (Assessment of Environmental Effects) (No. 2) Regulations 1989 (SI No. 424)
- Highways (Assessment of Environmental Effects) Regulations 1988 (SI No. 1241)
- Electricity and Pipe-line Works (Assessment of Environmental Effects) Regulations 1990 (SI No. 442)

Scotland:

- Environmental Assessment (Scotland) Regulations 1988 (SI No. 1221)
- Town and Country Planning (General Development) (Scotland) Amendment Order 1988 (SI No. 997)
- Town and Country Planning (General Development) (Scotland) Amendment No. 2 Order 1988 (SI No. 1249)

Northern Ireland:

- Planning (Assessment of Environmental Effects) Regulations (Northern Ireland) 1989 (SR No. 20)
- Environmental Assessment (Afforestation) Regulations (Northern Ireland) 1989 (SR No. 226)
- Roads (Assessment of Environmental Effects) Regulations (Northern Ireland) 1988 (SR No. 344)
- Harbour Works (Assessment of Environmental Effects) Regulations (Northern Ireland) 1990 (SR No. 181)

Appendix 3: An Example of a Typical Environmental Statement

Guidance Note:

This environmental statement is a compilation of three similar statements obtained in the course of compiling this work. Details have been revised and names changed to maintain anonymity. It is representative of typical environmental statements but it is not suggested that this be used as a pro-forma document as it displays a number of detailed weaknesses as outlined in Chapter 6.

ABC
OFFICE
DEVELOPMENT

A Planning Application
by
ABC Developments Plc

ENVIRONMENTAL
STATEMENT

Prepared by:
Smith, Jones & Partners
Environmental Assessment

CONTENTS:

1.0   INTRODUCTION

1.1   This Environmental Statement refers to our proposed planning application to develop a new purpose built office complex at Redland Hill to the east of Redland. At present, ABC Developments Plc occupy a building at West Redland dating back to 1937. These premises, however, no longer offer suitable accommodation. An owner for the present premises has, tentatively, been secured.

1.2   A development study commissioned by ABC Developments Plc investigated two options; to refurbish and extend the existing premises at West Redland, or to develop a new purpose built office at the site in East Redland. The environmental assessment specialist Smith, Jones and Partners was appointed to undertake an environmental assessment of the second proposal. This Environmental Statement reports the findings of that assessment.

2.0   THE CONTRIBUTION OF ENVIRONMENTAL ASSESSMENT

2.1   This proposal is not subject to environmental assessment, as set out in the Town and Country Planning (Assessment of Environmental Effects) Regulations (1988). However, through its commitment to considering environmental protection of new development projects, ABC Developments Plc has commissioned such environmental assessment to advise the design team and ensure that the resulting development represents the best environmental option available.

2.2   The environmental assessment sets out to address aspects of the environment likely to be significantly sensitive to the proposed development, to evaluate impacts which are likely to arise, to establish opportunities either through the building's siting or design to minimise them, and finally to assess the significance of any residual environmental effects of the development in use.

3.0   THE NATURE OF THE SITE

3.1   The site is located to the east of Redland Hill and next to Redland Wood with access from the A421 and B764 (Redland Lane). The site is roughly rectangular in shape, extends to 42 acres (17 ha) and slopes gently from south east to north west. The eastern boundary is made up of a small wooded valley. This joins the larger Redland Wood which forms the northern and north eastern elevations of the site. The site slopes down towards the Black Water River which runs at the base of the valley. The north western bank of the valley is woodland and considered to be of important conservation value.

3.2   There are two Ancient Monuments near to the site, Redland Hill Fort to the north east, and Redland Burial Mound which is directly adjacent to the eastern edge of the site.

3.3   Other significant development in the direct vicinity includes the Redland Agricultural Centre to the south west and Redland Olde Coaching Inn to the north west. The small village of Blackwater with some 30 properties, lies further to the west. At present the site is owned by ABC Developments Plc, acquired some 3 years ago for planned development.

* A site plan would generally accompany the descriptive information.

4.0   SCOPE OF THE ENVIRONMENTAL ASSESSMENT

4.1   In identifying the primary environmental issues, matters and concerns to which the development proposals give rise, various discussions and site meetings were held with both statutory and non-statutory consultees with a particular interest in the proposals.

4.2   On the basis of discussions, the following issues were identified:

- planning and land use implications.
- ecological aspects.
- landscape and visual issues.
- impacts on natural water resources.
- aspects of archaeological interest.
- ground conditions.
- traffic impact.
- noise impacts.
- construction influences.

5.0   ENVIRONMENTAL IMPACT

5.1   *Planning and Land Use Implications*

5.1.1 The proposed office development is well supported by local planning policy. A Notice of Intention to Develop submitted to Redland District

Council was unopposed by the Council and the various consultees to the Notice.

5.1.2 Impacts on land use are shown to be minimal. At present the primary land use at the site is agricultural. Almost 70% is grazing land, leased by ABC developments Plc to local farmers. Its loss to the development will not be significant; in fact alternative grazing facilities have been discussed and agreed.

5.1.3 Other features of the site which would regrettably be lost directly are two hedgerows which cross the field in a north-east–south-west direction and several trees. There are no existing leisure facilities on the site, although Redland District Council presently has proposals to develop a forest and riverside walk at Blackwater. It is not considered that this will pose any difficulty to the proposed development, in fact ABC Development Plc will part-fund this where appropriate.

5.2   *Ecological Aspects*

5.2.1 The wooded slope of the Blackwater Valley and of the smaller adjoining valley are both of local nature conservation importance in that they comprise sections of recognised ancient woodland with their associated flora and fauna. These aspects are recognised in proposals by Redland District Council to designate the area as a Key Site for Nature Conservation in its local plan. No other aspects of significant conservation importance have been identified in connection with this site. Providing public access into these areas is restricted the proposals will not give rise to detrimental ecological impacts of major significance.

5.2.2 Construction activities will give rise to some impact, however, the most important being potential ground water run-off from the site carrying possible contamination such as waste, diesel, petrol, oils, etc. during construction. Strict environmental management control during the construction phase will ensure these impacts are kept to a minimum.

5.3   *Landscape and Visual Issues*

5.3.1 The site is not located in a designated landscape area although the character of both Redland and Blackwater and the surrounding environs should be considered as features of local landscape value. In the context of existing development in the area, however, development of the site is not considered to have a significant landscape impact. The site is naturally well screened.

5.3.2 Views onto the site are already very limited. The visibility of the complex will be further limited by its low profile, by sensitive landscaping and the strengthening of existing vegetation at the site boundaries to complement the surrounding features. Much is wooded, sufficiently hiding the proposed development.

5.4   *Impacts on Natural Water Resources*

5.4.1 The Black Water River is the natural reception for discharges off-site. It tends to be of low quality, typical of water courses in rural/urban areas which are subject to many pollution sources from roads and development sites. Discharges will be limited to surface run-off from areas of hard-standing and buildings. These will drain separately, the former via oil and grit interceptors and the latter directly to the Black Water.

5.4.2 All discharges will be controlled by the Redland Water Board under consent. The development proposals include provision of sewerage which will link the development with the existing sewage treatment works at East Redland. The Redland Regional Council Sewage Department has confirmed that there is sufficient capacity at these works to accommodate the new development.

5.5   *Aspects of Archaeological Interest*

5.5.1 Redland Hill fort and Redland Hill Burial Mound, both listed Ancient Monuments protected by statute, are near to the site. Redland Hill fort is some 250 metres north east beyond the Black Water whilst the Burial Mound is immediately to the east of the site. Neither Monument will be directly affected by the development.

5.5.2 The development provides an opportunity to promote the archaeological interest of the site. A number of recommendations in this regard are outlined subsequently.

5.6   *Ground Conditions*

5.6.1 The site is not suspected to give rise to significant ground contamination. In the east some 10 metres from the site's eastern boundary is a former private quarry/mine. This was infilled in the 1950s. The source of fill material is unknown although it is suspected to be predominantly building rubble from nearby construction work in Redland. The possibility of landfill cannot be ruled out but is not considered to a major hazard in this case. Ground conditions do not pose any significant hazard to the project or its environs. Further investigation may be appropriate to determine the precise nature of ground fill materials.

5.7   Traffic Impact

5.7.1   The impacts of traffic associated with the development have been considered with respect to both noise and air quality. Impacts on the road network are not addressed here as they are part of an on-going appraisal by Redland Regional Council Roads Department. Both traffic noise and air quality impacts have been addressed at the nearest sensitive receptors, namely the Redland Agricultural Centre and Blackwater Village.

5.7.2   It is believed that the anticipated peak number of vehicles entering and leaving the office development will be some 70 to 90 vehicles (between 08.00 and 09.15 and 16.45 and 17.15). It is assumed that 80% will travel to and from the west of the site and 20% from the east. This will increase peak traffic flow on the A421 and Redland Lane but not significantly as flexible working times are envisaged.

5.7.3   The increase in traffic noise associated with the additional traffic is anticipated to be between 3 and 5 dB and this increase is not significant and will not affect the surrounding environs.

5.7.4   Air pollutants from traffic diminishes significantly with increasing distance from the main road. The increase in traffic will add only marginally to the levels of vehicle emissions. Increases will be extremely small and levels will remain within appropriate air quality criteria. Air pollution is therefore not considered a problem to the local environment.

5.8   Noise Impacts

5.8.1   There are few features sensitive to noise impacts in the vicinity of the site, although Blackwater Village and Redland Agricultural Centre are close by. Sources of noise arising from the completed development is limited to vehicle movements associated with the office staff and visitors. The present noise climate is dominated by noise arising predominantly from the Redland Agricultural Centre and the nearby farms. In view of the low existing and expected ambient noise conditions noise impacts are considered insignificant.

5.8.2   The relatively low levels of ambient noise are significant, however, in that special consideration will need to be given to the design, orientation and construction of the office car parks to ensure that acceptable low standards of noise within the environs are maintained at peak arrival and departure times although overall noise is not considered a major problem.

5.9   *Construction*

5.9.1 Construction at the site will give rise to typical construction impacts such as noise, dust, surface run-off, waste disposal, etc. However, they should be seen in the context of their limited and temporary duration and the existing construction activities elsewhere in the vicinity of the site. Attention to site environmental management and codes of construction practice will help to alleviate potential short-term problems. There will be no residual effects from the construction process.

6.0   MITIGATION OF ENVIRONMENTAL EFFECTS

This section summarises recommendations, arising from the environmental assessment, aimed at mitigating the potential environmental impacts of the project.

6.1   *Building Design*

Attention to the design, orientation and construction of the building will help to alleviate a number of potential environmental impacts, for example:

6.1.1 Restrictive development: a conscious attempt should be made to ensure that the profile and layout of built development harmonise with the surroundings and the heights be kept to a minimum. This will avoid unnecessary visual and other disturbance to the site and will reduce on site costs.

6.1.2 Low building profile: a low building profile should be achieved. The current proposal is to limit the height of the complex to a single or two storey, this will help to keep the visibility of the development to a minimum. A low rise development will be well screened by the natural environment. The building will not be seen from any surrounding perspective.

6.1.3 External noise levels: items of fixed plant such as air conditioning equipment should be oriented away from sensitive off-site or on-site features. Consideration may also be given to enclosing particularly noisy machinery or plant which generates 'tonal' noise.

6.1.4 Internal noise levels: consideration should be given to building materials and designs which provide sufficient attenuation that acceptable standards of indoor noise can be achieved. Sensitive positioning and orientation of the offices within the site, optimising the distance between the development and the A421 and maximising the attenuating effect of the site's topography should also be taken into account.

6.2 Site Layout

Environmental impacts can be controlled through attention to the layout of the site.

6.2.1 Landscaping proposals: landscaping and revegetation proposals will fulfil both a visual and ecological function. Proposals should include strengthening existing planting at the perimeter of the site and the recreation of the natural habitat lost by the removal of the two hedgerows and trees. Planting should attempt to recreate a vegetation structure which blends with the natural woodland and should employ local indigenous plants and tree species to meet with existing.

6.2.2 Drainage: all surface drainage from roads, car parks and hard-surfaced areas should be collected via a planned drainage network. Grit interceptors and oil traps should be installed at the frequency (per number of car parking spaces) recommended by the Redland River Board. Clean run-off from buildings may be run directly to the receiving water courses.

6.3 Construction

Construction impacts should be controlled by planned environmental site management. Control should be formalised through a series of environmental management practices which could be incorporated into terms of contract with the main contractor. The following measures should be addressed by site management:

6.3.1 Noise control: items of construction plant should be fitted with silencers and attenuated at source. Where possible, they should be located away from sensitive areas such as farming areas. Noise from activities such as excavating should be minimised. General construction noise disturbance will be minimised by imposing restrictions on the hours of working.

6.3.2 Dust control: dust control should be achieved by restricting vehicle movements to hard-surfaced site access roads. Wheel washing and road spraying will also minimise dust.

6.3.3 Run-off: drainage should be prevented by excavating cut-off drains protecting the Black Water River. Storage areas for fuel, and other hazardous materials, should be concrete lined and bunded to prevent the escape of accidental spillages.

6.4   *Environmental Opportunities*

The development provides a number of opportunities to promote certain features of the site in a positive way.

6.4.1 Archaeological interest: if the opportunity exists, this could be developed by providing an information or interpretation facility explaining the characteristics and interest of the two Ancient Monuments listed. The local authority and ABC Developments Plc are reviewing this aspect.

6.4.2 Ecological interest: a similar idea could be followed to set out the local conservation interest of the woodland. This would complement the District Council's proposals to develop a forest walk alongside the river. Combining the recreational and ecological resources in this way would help to provide a valuable area of 'ecological amenity', of benefit both to employees of ABC Developments Plc and the local community. Again ABC Developments Plc are liaising with the District Council to discuss this at this time.

7.0   SOURCES OF FURTHER INFORMATION

Further information concerning this environmental statement may be obtained from: Smith, Jones & Partners (Environmental Assessment).

Appendix 4: Outline Case Study in Environmental Assessment

Introduction

This case study focuses upon the environmental assessment for a new trunk road (by-pass) project. It describes the legislation applicable to its development, the procedures used and the issues arising from the assessment process.

Legislative background

Motorways and other major trunk road schemes (in England and Wales) are assessed for their potential environmental impact under the Highways (Assessment of Environmental Effects) Regulations 1988. The established procedures allow for the consideration of the potential effects of the proposed project upon both the human and environmental elements whilst considering the technical and financial aspects of the development. Under EC Directive 85/337/EEC, the procedures may be evaluated, upon referral, by the European Commission who may judge alleged failure to meet with and implement the Directive.

Requirements for an environmental statement

When a preferred route has been determined for a new motorway or trunk road scheme statutory orders will be published, where upon the scheme may become the subject of a public enquiry. The Highways (Assessment of Environmental Effects) Regulations 1988 require the Secretary of State to publish an environmental statement for the selected route when the draft statutory orders are published.

Such a requirement applies to all new motorways and trunk roads over 10 kilometres in length or roads which exceed 1 kilometre where the route passes through or intrudes within 100 metres of a recognised area of sensitivity.

An environmental statement is also pre-requisite for trunk road improvements which are likely to have a major effect upon the surrounding environs. Specific statutory bodies must be consulted where the road lies within or intrudes within 100 metres of a designated environmentally sensitive area. In

219

all cases, the environmental statement should be published and any comments generated should be considered at a public enquiry should one occur.

Project characteristics

The case study project was a proposed by-pass development, exceeding 1 kilometre and sited within 100 metres of an established village. The project, whilst not being sensitive in terms of its proposed scale and constitution, was considered environmentally sensitive because of its intrusion upon the existing site of human habitation and since the area does retain minor archaeological and historic interests, together with woodland, flora and fauna deemed to be of important social value to the local community.

Issues raised during environmental assessment

Although it was generally considered that the benefits of the proposed by-pass outweighed the limited environmental effects that would be incurred, a full environmental impact assessment was conducted on the proposed site and within the environs. This focused upon the disturbance to the visual landscape from proposed cuttings and embankments, the drainage scheme associated with the road construction and the effect of removing established trees, hedges and shrubs that sheltered the neighbouring village. Attention was also drawn to the potential requirements for noise attenuation as the by-pass was to run close to a part of the village.

Mitigating measures

Particular mitigating measures were identified in the resulting environmental statement. These included: changes in design to the embankments which needed to be higher in particular locations; the identified need for additional screening between the village and the new road, to be provided by natural hedging and dense tree belts; and detail changes to fencing and siting of bus-stops and pedestrian walkways.

Outcome

On the case study project, planning permission was, of course, not required as trunk roads and motorways are not subject to planning control.

Following the designated procedures this project was subsequently developed and successfully constructed. The scheme is now an accepted feature in the local community and there appears to be no residual effects to the local or wider environment or community.

Comment and discussion

The resounding success of the case study project should not lead one to believe that all projects are as effectively planned, assessed and constructed. A considerable number of construction developments are, in fact, referred annually to the European Commission under Directive 85/337/EEC where it is suggested that there has been infringement of the Directive. Planning permission is, on occasion, seemingly granted before complete and comprehensive information is acquired and documentation presented. Also, on some construction projects, it is likely that project development does, in fact, go too far down the road before a public enquiry, to be altered. Projects are committed without all the environmental issues being identified and considered. This, of course, raises the issue of just how much commitment there is to environmental assessment legislation or, perhaps more significantly, to the protection of the environment.

Such problems might be overcome, or at least there could be some attempt at mitigation if environmental assessment was to become part of a higher decision-making process, i.e. to a strategic planning and control level, but, at present, there is little support to determining environmental assessment as an intrinsic part of national policy and planning.

In conclusion, it must be said that whilst environmental assessment is a useful management tool to be employed in protecting the environment, there is a long way to go until it is perfected and complete reliance be placed upon it.

Appendix 5: Criteria for Construction Projects Requiring Environmental Assessment

Preamble

This section outlines those criteria for determining the need for environmental assessment. The reader is directed to authoritative documentation for the precise requirements and detailed information.

Urban development projects

The need for environmental assessment is determined by the sensitivity of the specific location. Schemes (other than housing schemes) may require an environmental assessment where:

- Site area of the scheme exceeds 5 ha in an urban area.
- There are dwellings close to the site.
- The development (shops, offices, etc.) exceeds 10,000 sq.m.

Smaller developments may require environmental assessment in particularly sensitive areas, for example those with historic interest. Out of town developments must also consider sensitivity of the scheme as a main criteria for assessment.

Industrial estate projects

Industrial estate developments may require an environmental assessment where:

- The site exceeds 20 ha.
- There are a considerable number of dwellings (over 1000).
- Dwellings are close to the site boundary (within 200 metres).

Manufacturing and industrial projects

Manufacturing installations may require environmental assessment where:

- Installations exceed 20 ha.
- There is likely to be pollution or other emissions.

- There might be discharge to water.
- There is any human hazard.

Highway projects

Motorways and trunk roads are not subject to planning control. Procedures for their constitution are set out in specific Acts of Parliament. The Highways (Assessment of Environmental Effects) Regulations 1988 require an environmental statement to be published for projects with specific characteristics:

- All new motorways and trunk roads exceeding 10 km.
- All new motorways and trunk roads exceeding 1 km, where the route passes through or within 100m of a sensitive area.

Where roads pass within 100m of environmentally sensitive areas, statutory bodies must be consulted before the project is initiated.

Roads

Other than new motorways and trunk roads, roads may require environmental assessment where:

- The road exceeds 10 km in length.
- The road is over 1 km and passes within a designated area of specified interest, i.e. a conservation area.
- The road is within 100 metres of a substantial number (1500) of dwellings.

Power stations

Power stations and overhead electricity supplies are not subject to planning control. They are controlled by the Secretary of State for Energy. An environmental statement is prerequisite where:

- A nuclear power station is to be constructed or extended.
- A non-nuclear power station is proposed exceeding 300 megawatts.
- A power station is likely to give rise to significant environmental effects.
- An overhead power line may have significant environmental effects.

Appendix 6: Contractor's Environmental Site Survey Checklist

Guidance Note:

An environmental site survey enables the contractor to make a first-hand, on-site assessment of the potential and in some cases the actual sources of environmental effects. The survey should cover aspects such as spillages; discharges; contamination; emission; waste control; and health and safety. Some examples are presented in this appendix.

An important function of the survey is to identify previously unreported or overlooked aspects of potential environmental effect which may not have been recorded in the developer's environmental statement or in the contractor's own tender site investigation.

To ensure that the environmental site survey encompasses all aspects of potential environmental impact, it should be undertaken in logical sections. As identified in Chapter 7, the survey may examine by (i) route of emission or (ii) by area approach. In either form, a checklist of items will aid evaluation.

(i) Spillage prevention and control

Spillages may lead to air and water pollution and also the contamination of land on the site. It is therefore essential to identify the potential for spillage or hazardous substances and to consider possible action to mitigate potential environmental effects. The following should be achieved:

- Identify all potential substances (liquids, fuels, etc.) that will be brought onto site and list, describe and quantify same.
- Determine approximate frequency of delivery and designate delivery locations.
- Examine the integrity of storage and containment areas.
- Anticipate the potential route of spillage if it should occur.
- Determine effective monitoring mechanisms to identify spillage during delivery, storage and handling procedures.
- Consider any hidden sources of spillage or run-off.
- Assess the potential for spillage elsewhere on site during delivery, i.e. from tankers, etc.

- Anticipate spillage contamination to existing drainage runs, water courses and water supplies.
- Consider possible modification to any planned measures to improve efficiency in operations.

(ii) Discharges

Water pollution as a result of discharges usually occur within the categories of: sanitary waste water; process water; wash-down water; and rainwater/stormwater leading to site run-off. When conducting the environmental site survey the following should be achieved:

- Identify all potential sources of water pollution on site.
- Determine the presence of existing drainage and inspect.
- Consider new permanent and temporary site drainage installations.
- Examine all outfalls, natural or man-made and inspect for existing pollutants.
- Assess the potential for run-off during heavy rain/storm and determine hazard potential of run-off pollutants.
- Check any existing drains against site plan for true location and test for integrity.
- Assess the potential of harmful discharge if an environmental effect occurs on site.
- Consider the effect of site processes upon water discharge, i.e. plant washing facilities, etc.
- Determine water segregation systems, i.e. sanitary, wash-down, surface water, etc.
- Check the cleanliness of water supply and distribution.
- Consider any water storage requirements on site.

(iii) Contamination

Contamination of land may occur both directly and indirectly with the most common cause being spillages and waste dumping. When conducting an environmental site survey the following should be achieved:

- Determine if the site is already contaminated by previous use. If so, define, describe and quantify.
- Identify all potential sources of contamination from site activities.
- Consider the requirement for removing potential contaminant material off-site.
- Assess handling, storage and contaminant areas whilst awaiting removal from site.
- Determine effective monitoring procedures to check status of such materials.

- Anticipate the potential nature and route of effect if it should occur: i.e. seepage into ground, air emission raining on site, etc.

(iv) Health and safety

Basic requirements for the management of health and safety on site which should be considered during the environmental site survey include the following aspects which should form the core of the health and safety plan:

- Determine the project requirements as communicated in the planning supervisor's health and safety plan.
- Identify all potential risks and hazards associated with site activities.
- Assign responsibilities to key site personnel.
- Ensure monitoring mechanisms are in place for each aspect identified.
- Determine actions, resources and mechanisms needed should an incident occur.
- Formalise recording mechanisms at project and statutory level.

Appendix 7: Sources of Further Information

Environmental management systems

British Standards Institution (BSI)
Linford Wood
Milton Keynes MK14 6LE

British Standards Institution (BSI)
2 Park Street
London W1A 2BS

(BS 7750: Specification for Environmental Management Systems)

European Directives and Environmental Management Initiatives

Department of the Environment (DoE)
Construction Policy Directorate
Romney House
43 Marsham Street
London SW1P 3PY

Environmental assessment

Department of Environment (DoE)
Construction Policy Directorate
Romney House
43 Marsham Street
London SW1P 3PY

Environmental Assessment: A Guide to the Procedures, HMSO (1989)
(available from HMSO bookshops and booksellers).

Index